CONTENTS

Quantum Encryption: Unlocking the Future of Secure Communication — 1

Introduction — 2

Overview of Quantum Encryption — 3

The Evolution of Encryption Methods: From Classical to Quantum — 5

The Need for Quantum Encryption in the Era of Quantum Computing — 7

Key Objectives of the Book — 9

Structure of the Book — 10

Chapter 1: Introduction to Quantum Mechanics — 12

Fundamental Principles of Quantum Mechanics — 13

Measurement and the Observer Effect — 15

Relevance of Quantum Mechanics to Encryption — 16

Mathematical Frameworks for Quantum States and Operators — 17

Conclusion — 19

Chapter 2: Basics of Classical Encryption — 20

Overview of Classical Encryption Techniques — 21

Prominent Classical Encryption Algorithms — 23

Limitations of Classical Encryption in the Face of Quantum Computing — 25

Transitioning from Classical to Quantum-Safe Methods   27

Conclusion   29

Chapter 3: Quantum Cryptography   30

Differences Between Classical and Quantum Cryptography   31

Key Principles of Quantum Cryptography   33

Security Implications of Quantum Cryptography   35

Conclusion   37

Chapter 4: Quantum Key Distribution (QKD)   38

Theoretical Foundation of QKD   39

Security Proof of QKD Systems   42

Practical Considerations and Limitations   45

Conclusion   47

Chapter 5: Post-Quantum Cryptography   48

Definition and Principles of Post-Quantum Cryptography   49

Comparison with Quantum Cryptography   51

Algorithms Designed for Post-Quantum Resilience   52

Conclusion   56

Chapter 6: Quantum Random Number Generation (QRNG)   57

Importance of Randomness in Cryptographic Systems   58

QRNG Mechanisms Using Quantum Mechanics   60

Comparison of QRNG with Classical Random Number Generators   62

Applications of QRNG   64

Conclusion   65

Chapter 7: Building a Quantum Key Distribution Network   66

Components of a QKD System   67

Hardware Requirements   69

Use Cases and Existing QKD Networks   73

Challenges in Building QKD Networks   76

Conclusion   77

Chapter 8: Securing Communications with Quantum Encryption   78

Implementation of Quantum Encryption in Secure Messaging Systems   79

Implementation of Quantum Encryption in Virtual Private Networks (VPNs)   83

Protocols for Integrating QKD with Classical Encryption   85

Conclusion   89

Chapter 9: Quantum-Secure Cloud Storage   90

Framework for Applying Quantum Encryption in Cloud Services   91

Ensuring End-to-End Encryption with QKD   93

Challenges in Scalability and Cost-Effectiveness   95

Real-World Applications and Examples   97

Conclusion   98

Chapter 10: Quantum Blockchain and Decentralized Systems   99

Integration of Quantum Encryption into Blockchain Technology   100

Quantum-Resistant Consensus Mechanisms   103

Applications in Decentralized Finance (DeFi) and Identity Management   105

Challenges and Future Directions   107

Conclusion   108

Chapter 11: Hybrid Encryption Frameworks   109

Combining Classical and Quantum Encryption Methods   110

Designing Hybrid Systems for Gradual Transition to Quantum-Safe Encryption   113

Case Studies on Hybrid Frameworks in Industries 115

Challenges and Future Directions 118

Conclusion 120

Chapter 12: Quantum Encryption in IoT Systems 121

Challenges of Securing IoT Devices 122

Framework for Implementing Lightweight Quantum Encryption 124

Practical Solutions for IoT Ecosystems 127

Case Studies 130

Challenges and Future Directions 132

Conclusion 135

Chapter 13: Quantum Encryption in Military and Government Applications 136

High-Security Applications of Quantum Encryption 137

Quantum-Resistant Frameworks for National Defense 141

Ethical and Geopolitical Implications 143

Case Studies 145

Challenges and Future Directions 147

Conclusion 149

Chapter 14: Hardware for Quantum Encryption 150

Essential Quantum Hardware Components 151

Current Market Solutions 154

Future Trends in Quantum Encryption Hardware 156

Challenges in Hardware Development 158

Conclusion 159

Chapter 15: Software Frameworks for Quantum Encryption 160

Open-Source Quantum Encryption Libraries 161

Developing Custom Encryption Software 164

Integrating Quantum Encryption APIs   167

Future Trends in Quantum Encryption Software   169

Conclusion   171

Chapter 16: Building Quantum-Resistant Systems Today   172

Roadmap for Transitioning to Quantum-Safe Infrastructure   173

Adapting Current Systems to Incorporate Quantum Encryption   176

Framework for Small Businesses and Enterprise-Level Implementation   179

Case Studies   183

Conclusion   185

Chapter 17: Testing and Validating Quantum Encryption Systems   186

Standards and Protocols for Testing Quantum Encryption   187

Simulating Attacks to Evaluate Robustness   190

Certification and Compliance with International Standards   192

Case Studies   194

Challenges and Future Directions   197

Conclusion   198

Chapter 18: The Future of Quantum Encryption   199

Trends in Quantum Encryption Research   200

The Potential Role of Artificial Intelligence in Quantum Systems   202

Speculative Applications and Technological Milestones   204

Technological Milestones in Quantum Encryption   206

Challenges and Considerations   208

Conclusion   209

Chapter 19: Ethical and Societal Implications of Quantum Encryption 210

Balancing Privacy and Surveillance in a Quantum-Secure World 211

Preventing Misuse of Quantum Encryption Technologies 213

Global Cooperation in the Quantum Age 215

Case Studies 218

Conclusion 220

Conclusion: Embracing Quantum Security 221

Summary of Key Insights from the Book 222

Call to Action for Businesses, Governments, and Individuals 224

The Promise of Quantum Encryption 226

Final Thoughts 228

QUANTUM ENCRYPTION: UNLOCKING THE FUTURE OF SECURE COMMUNICATION

By

Tony Yustein © 2024
https://thecode.wiki

INTRODUCTION

Quantum Encryption: Unlocking the Future of Secure Communication

• •

OVERVIEW OF QUANTUM ENCRYPTION

In a world increasingly reliant on digital infrastructure, the security of information is paramount. From personal communications to global financial systems, data security forms the backbone of modern society. However, as technology advances, so do the methods of breaching these systems. Enter **quantum encryption**—a revolutionary approach poised to redefine how we protect our digital world.

Quantum encryption leverages the principles of quantum mechanics to ensure unparalleled security. Unlike classical encryption, which relies on mathematical complexity to deter attackers, quantum encryption employs the fundamental properties of particles at the quantum level, such as superposition and entanglement, to safeguard information. These principles render quantum encryption theoretically impervious to eavesdropping and brute-force attacks, setting a new standard for secure communication.

This technology is not just a response to current security challenges but also a proactive measure against the imminent threat posed by quantum computing. As quantum computers grow in capability, they will render many traditional encryption methods obsolete, leaving our most sensitive data vulnerable. Quantum encryption, with its ability to utilize quantum key distribution (QKD) and other cutting-edge techniques, offers a robust defense for the future.

THE EVOLUTION OF ENCRYPTION METHODS: FROM CLASSICAL TO QUANTUM

The journey of encryption is as old as the need to protect secrets. Classical encryption methods, from the substitution ciphers of antiquity to the sophisticated algorithms like RSA and AES of the digital age, have evolved in response to increasingly complex security needs. These methods rely on computational difficulty —mathematical problems so intricate that they would take conventional computers millions of years to solve.

However, this foundation is under siege with the advent of quantum computing. Quantum computers can perform calculations exponentially faster than classical systems, posing a direct threat to encryption techniques that depend on factorization, discrete logarithms, or elliptic curve mathematics. A quantum computer, equipped with algorithms like Shor's algorithm, could unravel these once-impenetrable codes in seconds.

Quantum encryption represents a paradigm shift. Instead of building defenses based on computational hardness, it employs the unassailable principles of quantum mechanics. For example, the no-cloning theorem ensures that quantum information cannot be copied, making eavesdropping detectable. This marks a turning point in the history of encryption—one where we move beyond reactive measures to proactive security rooted in the fundamental laws of nature.

• •

THE NEED FOR QUANTUM ENCRYPTION IN THE ERA OF QUANTUM COMPUTING

The quantum computing revolution is both an opportunity and a challenge. On one hand, it promises breakthroughs in fields such as medicine, materials science, and artificial intelligence. On the other hand, it poses an existential threat to current encryption systems. Without adequate preparation, the onset of quantum computing could lead to a catastrophic breach of global data security.

Quantum encryption addresses this challenge head-on. By integrating quantum key distribution (QKD) and quantum random number generation (QRNG) into communication systems, it ensures secure transmission even against quantum-capable adversaries. The implementation of these technologies today is crucial to building a resilient digital infrastructure for tomorrow.

Beyond quantum computing, quantum encryption addresses the growing need for privacy in a world of pervasive surveillance and increasing cyber threats. By combining theoretical security with practical applications, it represents a holistic solution to the evolving demands of cybersecurity.

KEY OBJECTIVES
OF THE BOOK

This book is designed to:

1. Provide a comprehensive understanding of quantum encryption, from its theoretical underpinnings to practical implementations.

2. Explore the evolution of encryption, highlighting the limitations of classical methods and the necessity of quantum-safe alternatives.

3. Equip readers with actionable knowledge to implement quantum encryption systems using today's technology.

4. Present a forward-looking perspective on the future of encryption in the quantum era, addressing both opportunities and challenges.

5. Bridge the gap between theoretical concepts and real-world applications, making quantum encryption accessible to both experts and enthusiasts.

• •

STRUCTURE OF THE BOOK

To achieve these objectives, the book is organized into six parts, each building upon the last to create a holistic understanding of quantum encryption:

1. **Foundations of Quantum Encryption:**
    Introduces the principles of quantum mechanics and classical encryption, setting the stage for quantum cryptography.

2. **Theory of Quantum Encryption:**
    Delves into key concepts such as quantum key distribution (QKD), post-quantum cryptography, and quantum random number generation (QRNG).

3. **Practical Applications of Quantum Encryption:**
    Demonstrates real-world use cases, including secure communication, quantum-secure cloud storage, and IoT systems.

4. **Advanced Topics and Frameworks:**
    Explores cutting-edge applications like quantum blockchain, hybrid encryption systems, and military uses.

5. **Implementation Frameworks:**
    Provides actionable steps for integrating quantum encryption into existing systems, covering both hardware and software requirements.

6. **Future Directions and Ethical Considerations:**

Examines the future of quantum encryption, its societal implications, and the ethical challenges it presents.

Each chapter alternates between theory and practical applications to ensure a balanced approach. By the end of the book, readers will not only understand quantum encryption but also possess the tools to implement it in diverse scenarios.

• •

Quantum encryption is not just the next step in data security —it is a leap into a future where communication can be truly secure. This book invites you to embark on a journey through this transformative field, exploring its potential to redefine how we protect information in the quantum era.

CHAPTER 1: INTRODUCTION TO QUANTUM MECHANICS

Quantum mechanics is the cornerstone of modern physics and serves as the foundation for quantum encryption. Its principles defy classical intuition, offering a new lens through which we understand the universe. In this chapter, we delve into the fundamental principles of quantum mechanics, their relevance to encryption, and the mathematical frameworks that make them applicable to real-world technologies.

• •

FUNDAMENTAL PRINCIPLES OF QUANTUM MECHANICS

Superposition

Superposition is the principle that a quantum system can exist in multiple states simultaneously until measured. For example, a quantum bit (qubit) can exist in a state of $|0\rangle$, $|1\rangle$, or any linear combination of the two: $|\psi\rangle = \alpha|0\rangle + \beta|1\rangle$ where α and β are complex probability amplitudes, and $|\alpha|^2 + |\beta|^2 = 1$. This property enables quantum computers to perform computations on vast amounts of data simultaneously, making classical brute-force attacks on encryption obsolete.

Entanglement

Entanglement is a phenomenon where two or more quantum particles become correlated such that the state of one particle instantly determines the state of the other, regardless of the distance between them. Mathematically, an entangled state of two qubits can be represented as: $|\psi\rangle = \frac{1}{\sqrt{2}}(|00\rangle + |11\rangle)$
This non-local correlation forms the backbone of quantum key distribution (QKD), as any attempt to intercept the entangled particles disrupts their states, making eavesdropping

detectable.

Wave-Particle Duality

Quantum objects exhibit both wave-like and particle-like behavior, depending on how they are observed. For instance, photons can interfere like waves in the double-slit experiment but also behave like discrete particles when detected. This duality is fundamental in technologies like quantum random number generators (QRNG), which rely on the probabilistic nature of quantum events.

• •

MEASUREMENT AND THE OBSERVER EFFECT

Quantum mechanics introduces the concept of measurement as an active process that alters the state of a quantum system. When a quantum system is measured, it collapses from a superposition into one of its basis states. For

$$|\psi\rangle = \alpha|0\rangle + \beta|1\rangle \quad \xrightarrow{\text{Measurement}} \quad |0\rangle \text{ or } |1\rangle$$

example: This collapse underpins the security of quantum encryption. In quantum key distribution, any attempt to measure or intercept quantum states during transmission causes detectable disturbances, ensuring the integrity of the communication channel.

The **observer effect** emphasizes the role of measurement in determining the outcome of quantum systems, making it a critical feature for designing secure quantum protocols.

• •

RELEVANCE OF QUANTUM MECHANICS TO ENCRYPTION

Quantum mechanics provides principles that fundamentally redefine security in communication systems:

1. **Quantum No-Cloning Theorem:** It is impossible to create an identical copy of an unknown quantum state. This guarantees that quantum keys cannot be duplicated by an attacker.

2. **Intrinsic Randomness:** Quantum events, such as the spin of a photon, are inherently random, enabling the generation of truly random keys.

3. **Detectable Interception:** Eavesdropping disrupts quantum states, making it evident to legitimate communicators.

These properties render quantum encryption resistant to attacks that would compromise classical encryption systems.

• •

MATHEMATICAL FRAMEWORKS FOR QUANTUM STATES AND OPERATORS

Understanding quantum mechanics requires a mathematical formalism grounded in linear algebra and complex numbers. Key components include:

Quantum States

Quantum states are represented as vectors in a complex vector space known as Hilbert space. For a single qubit: $|\psi\rangle = \begin{bmatrix} \alpha \\ \beta \end{bmatrix}$ where α and β are complex numbers.

Operators

Operators represent physical observables and transformations in quantum mechanics. For example, the Pauli operators for a qubit are:

$$X = \begin{bmatrix} 0 & 1 \\ 1 & 0 \end{bmatrix}, \quad Y = \begin{bmatrix} 0 & -i \\ i & 0 \end{bmatrix}, \quad Z = \begin{bmatrix} 1 & 0 \\ 0 & -1 \end{bmatrix}$$

These operators manipulate quantum states and are essential in building quantum encryption systems.

Quantum Gates

Quantum gates are unitary operators that transform quantum states. Common gates include:

- **Hadamard Gate (H):**
$$H = \frac{1}{\sqrt{2}}\begin{bmatrix} 1 & 1 \\ 1 & -1 \end{bmatrix}$$
This gate creates superposition states, a critical step in quantum key distribution.

$$CNOT = \begin{bmatrix} 1 & 0 & 0 & 0 \\ 0 & 1 & 0 & 0 \\ 0 & 0 & 0 & 1 \\ 0 & 0 & 1 & 0 \end{bmatrix}$$

- **Controlled-NOT Gate (CNOT):** This gate is used to entangle qubits.

Measurement Operators

Measurement collapses quantum states into classical outcomes. The projection operators for a qubit are: $P_0 = |0\rangle\langle 0|$, $P_1 = |1\rangle\langle 1|$ These operators extract the probabilities of the system collapsing into $|0\rangle$ or $|1\rangle$.

• •

CONCLUSION

This chapter has introduced the fundamental principles of quantum mechanics, including superposition, entanglement, and wave-particle duality, and their relevance to encryption. The observer effect and the mathematical frameworks for quantum states and operators provide the tools necessary for understanding and applying quantum encryption. As we move forward, these principles will serve as the foundation for exploring the theoretical and practical aspects of quantum encryption.

CHAPTER 2: BASICS OF CLASSICAL ENCRYPTION

Encryption is the cornerstone of data security in the digital age. Classical encryption techniques, rooted in mathematical principles, have safeguarded sensitive information for decades. This chapter provides an overview of the primary classical encryption techniques, explores prominent algorithms like RSA, AES, and elliptic-curve cryptography, examines their limitations in the era of quantum computing, and introduces the transition toward quantum-safe methods.

• •

OVERVIEW OF CLASSICAL ENCRYPTION TECHNIQUES

Classical encryption methods are broadly categorized into two types: **symmetric encryption** and **asymmetric encryption**. Each plays a critical role in securing communication, with unique strengths and weaknesses.

Symmetric Encryption

- **Definition:** In symmetric encryption, the same key is used for both encrypting and decrypting data.

- **Examples:** DES (Data Encryption Standard), AES (Advanced Encryption Standard).

- **Advantages:**

  - Faster computational speed compared to asymmetric encryption.

  - Simpler implementation.

- **Challenges:**

  - Key distribution is difficult, especially over insecure channels.

  - Scalability issues in large systems due to the need for unique keys between each pair of communicators.

Asymmetric Encryption

- **Definition:** Asymmetric encryption employs a pair of keys: a public key for encryption and a private key for decryption.

- **Examples:** RSA (Rivest-Shamir-Adleman), DSA (Digital Signature Algorithm), ECC (Elliptic-Curve Cryptography).

- **Advantages:**

  - Eliminates the need for secure key exchange.

  - Enables digital signatures for verifying data integrity and authenticity.

- **Challenges:**

  - Slower than symmetric encryption due to complex mathematical computations.

  - Vulnerable to attacks from sufficiently powerful computers, including quantum computers.

• •

PROMINENT CLASSICAL ENCRYPTION ALGORITHMS

RSA (Rivest-Shamir-Adleman)

- **How It Works:** RSA relies on the difficulty of factoring large composite numbers. The encryption key is derived from the product of two large prime numbers, while the private key is based on their unique factorization.

- **Key Features:**

  - Widely used for secure communications and digital signatures.

  - Security increases with key size (e.g., 2048-bit or 4096-bit keys).

- **Weaknesses:** Vulnerable to quantum attacks via Shor's algorithm, which can efficiently factorize large integers.

AES (Advanced Encryption Standard)

- **How It Works:** AES is a symmetric encryption algorithm based on the Rijndael cipher. It uses block sizes of 128 bits and key lengths of 128, 192, or 256 bits.

- **Key Features:**

  - Highly efficient for bulk data encryption.

- – Resistant to known classical attacks, such as brute force.

- **Weaknesses:** While not directly vulnerable to quantum attacks, AES requires longer key lengths (e.g., AES-256) to remain secure in the quantum era.

Elliptic-Curve Cryptography (ECC)

- **How It Works:** ECC uses the mathematical properties of elliptic curves over finite fields to create secure cryptographic keys. Its security relies on the difficulty of the elliptic-curve discrete logarithm problem (ECDLP).

- **Key Features:**

  - – Provides equivalent security to RSA with smaller key sizes (e.g., a 256-bit ECC key offers similar security to a 3072-bit RSA key).

  - – Ideal for devices with limited processing power, such as IoT devices.

- **Weaknesses:** Also susceptible to quantum attacks, as ECDLP can be solved efficiently using quantum computers.

· ·

LIMITATIONS OF CLASSICAL ENCRYPTION IN THE FACE OF QUANTUM COMPUTING

The advent of quantum computing threatens to render classical encryption methods obsolete. Quantum computers leverage principles such as superposition and entanglement to perform calculations exponentially faster than classical computers.

Key Threats from Quantum Computing

1. **Breaking Asymmetric Encryption:** Algorithms like Shor's algorithm can efficiently solve problems (e.g., integer factorization, discrete logarithms) that form the basis of RSA, DSA, and ECC.

2. **Impact on Symmetric Encryption:** While symmetric encryption remains more resilient, Grover's algorithm can reduce its effective key length by half. For instance, a 128-bit key offers only 64 bits of quantum-secure protection.

Implications

- Sensitive information encrypted today using classical methods could be decrypted in the future once quantum computers achieve sufficient capability.

- Organizations must begin transitioning to encryption methods that are resistant to quantum attacks.

· ·

TRANSITIONING FROM CLASSICAL TO QUANTUM-SAFE METHODS

To mitigate the risks posed by quantum computing, cryptographers are developing quantum-safe or post-quantum cryptographic algorithms. These methods aim to maintain security against both classical and quantum attacks.

Key Approaches to Quantum-Safe Cryptography

1. **Lattice-Based Cryptography:**
   Relies on the computational hardness of lattice problems, such as the Learning with Errors (LWE) problem. Algorithms include NTRUEncrypt and Kyber.

2. **Code-Based Cryptography:**
   Builds on the difficulty of decoding random linear codes. McEliece cryptosystem is a prominent example.

3. **Hash-Based Cryptography:**
   Uses cryptographic hash functions for secure signatures. Examples include Lamport signatures and Merkle trees.

4. **Multivariate Polynomial Cryptography:**
   Utilizes the complexity of solving multivariate polynomial equations.

5. **Hybrid Cryptographic Frameworks:**

Combines classical encryption with quantum-safe algorithms to enable a smoother transition.

Steps for Transition

1. **Assessment of Current Systems:**
   Evaluate existing encryption protocols for vulnerability to quantum attacks.

2. **Implementation of Quantum-Safe Algorithms:**
   Begin integrating post-quantum cryptography into communication systems.

3. **Standardization Efforts:**
   Follow guidelines from organizations like NIST (National Institute of Standards and Technology), which is actively developing post-quantum cryptographic standards.

• •

CONCLUSION

Classical encryption techniques, from symmetric encryption like AES to asymmetric methods like RSA and ECC, have been instrumental in securing digital communications. However, their limitations in the face of quantum computing necessitate a transition to quantum-safe alternatives. The development and adoption of post-quantum cryptography will ensure that secure communication can persist in the quantum era. This chapter has set the stage for understanding why quantum encryption is not just a technological advancement but a necessity for the future.

CHAPTER 3: QUANTUM CRYPTOGRAPHY

Quantum cryptography marks a paradigm shift in the field of secure communication, moving beyond the mathematical complexity of classical cryptography to the fundamental principles of quantum mechanics. This chapter explores the differences between classical and quantum cryptography, the key principles underpinning quantum cryptographic systems, and their far-reaching security implications.

• •

DIFFERENCES BETWEEN CLASSICAL AND QUANTUM CRYPTOGRAPHY

Classical cryptography relies on mathematical algorithms to secure communication. The security of these methods is based on computational difficulty, which becomes vulnerable in the presence of advanced computing technologies like quantum computers.

In contrast, quantum cryptography uses the laws of quantum mechanics to secure data. Rather than relying on the assumed difficulty of certain mathematical problems, it ensures security by leveraging the physical behavior of quantum particles, making it theoretically immune to brute-force attacks or computational advances.

Aspect	Classical Cryptography	Quantum Cryptography
Security Basis	Computational difficulty (e.g., factorization)	Physical laws of quantum mechanics
Key Exchange	Vulnerable to interception	Quantum key distribution (eavesdropping detectable)
Resistance to Attacks	Vulnerable to quantum computers	Immune to computational advancements
Randomness	Pseudo-random number generators	True randomness through quantum processes
Eavesdropping Detection	Not inherently detectable	Intrusion causes observable disturbances

Quantum cryptography addresses the inherent vulnerabilities

in classical systems, ensuring that security is maintained even in the face of quantum computing.

• •

KEY PRINCIPLES OF QUANTUM CRYPTOGRAPHY

1. Quantum No-Cloning Theorem

The quantum no-cloning theorem states that it is impossible to create an identical copy of an unknown quantum state. Mathematically, the theorem is derived from the linearity of quantum mechanics, which prevents perfect duplication: If $|\psi\rangle \neq |\phi\rangle$, then $|\psi\rangle$ and $|\phi\rangle$ cannot be cloned. This principle is critical for cryptography because it ensures that any attempt to copy a quantum key or message will fail, making quantum states inherently secure against interception.

- **Relevance to Cryptography:**
  When a quantum state is intercepted or measured, the original state collapses, altering the information in a detectable way. This ensures that communication systems can identify tampering or eavesdropping attempts.

2. Quantum Key Distribution (QKD)

Quantum key distribution is the cornerstone of quantum cryptography. It enables two parties to securely share a cryptographic key using quantum mechanics. The most widely known QKD protocol is **BB84**, named after its creators, Charles Bennett and Gilles Brassard (1984).

BB84 Protocol Overview

- **Preparation:**

The sender (Alice) prepares qubits in random quantum states, chosen from two bases (rectilinear or diagonal).

- **Transmission:**
Alice sends these qubits to the receiver (Bob) over a quantum channel.

- **Measurement:**
Bob measures the qubits using random bases.

- **Key Reconciliation:**
Alice and Bob compare their bases over a classical channel and discard non-matching results to form a shared key.

- **Error Detection:**
To detect eavesdropping, they compare a subset of the key. Any significant discrepancy indicates intrusion.

Device-Independent QKD

Device-independent QKD protocols ensure security even if the devices used are compromised. These protocols leverage quantum entanglement and Bell inequality violations to secure communication.

3. Entanglement-Based QKD

Entanglement-based QKD, such as the **E91 protocol** (developed by Artur Ekert in 1991), relies on entangled photon pairs. The security arises from the correlations between measurements of entangled particles, which are disrupted by any eavesdropping attempt.

• •

SECURITY IMPLICATIONS OF QUANTUM CRYPTOGRAPHY

Unconditional Security

Unlike classical cryptographic methods, whose security is conditional on computational hardness, quantum cryptography provides **unconditional security** based on the physical properties of quantum mechanics. This makes it immune to advances in computational power, including the development of quantum computers.

Resistance to Eavesdropping

The inherent properties of quantum mechanics ensure that any attempt to intercept or measure quantum states is detectable. In QKD, for instance, measurement disturbances caused by eavesdropping manifest as errors in the shared key, enabling the communicating parties to identify and reject compromised transmissions.

True Randomness

Quantum systems generate truly random numbers, as opposed to pseudo-random numbers produced by classical algorithms. This enhances the unpredictability and security of cryptographic keys.

Practical Applications

- **Military and Government Communications:**

Quantum cryptography is being adopted to secure sensitive communications in defense and intelligence sectors.

- **Banking and Finance:** Ensures secure transactions and protects against fraud.

- **Quantum-Secure Networks:** Large-scale networks, such as China's quantum satellite **Micius**, demonstrate the feasibility of implementing quantum cryptography on a global scale.

Limitations

While quantum cryptography offers unparalleled security, it faces practical challenges:

- **Infrastructure Requirements:** Quantum communication channels (e.g., fiber optics or satellite links) are necessary but expensive.

- **Distance Limitations:** Signal degradation over long distances limits the range of current QKD systems, though quantum repeaters and satellite-based QKD aim to address this.

• •

CONCLUSION

Quantum cryptography represents a revolutionary advancement in secure communication, grounded in the principles of quantum mechanics. By leveraging the quantum no-cloning theorem and quantum key distribution, it offers unparalleled protection against eavesdropping and computational attacks. While practical challenges remain, ongoing advancements in quantum technology promise to make quantum cryptography a cornerstone of secure communication in the digital age.

CHAPTER 4:
QUANTUM KEY
DISTRIBUTION (QKD)

Quantum Key Distribution (QKD) is a groundbreaking application of quantum mechanics that enables secure key exchange. Unlike classical methods, QKD ensures security through the fundamental principles of quantum physics, making it impervious to computational attacks. This chapter explores the theoretical foundation of QKD, focusing on the BB84 and E91 protocols, device-independent QKD, the security proof of QKD systems, and practical considerations for their implementation.

• •

THEORETICAL FOUNDATION OF QKD

Key Concept: Quantum Communication

QKD allows two parties, typically called Alice and Bob, to generate a shared secret key over an insecure channel while ensuring its security through quantum mechanics. The central idea is that any attempt to intercept or measure quantum states disturbs them, making eavesdropping detectable.

BB84 Protocol

The BB84 protocol, introduced by Charles Bennett and Gilles Brassard in 1984, is the first and most widely used QKD protocol. It operates using the principles of superposition and the no-cloning theorem.

Steps in the BB84 Protocol

1. **Key Encoding:**

   – Alice encodes random bits (0 or 1) onto the polarization states of photons using two randomly chosen bases: rectilinear ($+$) or diagonal ($\times$).

   – For example:

     • 0 in rectilinear basis: Horizontal polarization ($|\rangle$).

     • 1 in rectilinear basis: Vertical polarization ($|\uparrow\rangle$).

     • 0 in diagonal basis: 45° polarization ($|\nearrow\rangle$).

- • ^{1} in diagonal basis: 135° polarization ($|\searrow\rangle$).

2. **Transmission:**

– Alice sends these photons to Bob over a quantum channel.

3. **Key Measurement:**

– Bob measures the incoming photons using randomly chosen bases (rectilinear or diagonal).

4. **Basis Reconciliation:**

– Alice and Bob publicly share their chosen bases for each bit. Bob retains only the bits where their bases match.

5. **Error Detection:**

– Alice and Bob compare a subset of their key to detect potential eavesdropping.

6. **Key Generation:**

– If the error rate is below a certain threshold, the remaining bits are used to form the secret key.

· ·

E91 Protocol

The E91 protocol, developed by Artur Ekert in 1991, leverages quantum entanglement for key distribution. Entanglement-based QKD offers higher security by relying on the correlations between entangled particles.

Steps in the E91 Protocol

1. **Entangled Pair Generation:**

– A source generates pairs of entangled particles and sends one particle to Alice and the other to Bob.

2. **Measurement:**

– Alice and Bob measure their particles using randomly chosen bases.

3. **Correlation:**

– The results are compared, revealing strong correlations if the particles are entangled.

4. **Key Generation:**

– Alice and Bob use the correlated results to form a shared key.

Advantages of the E91 Protocol

• Security is derived from the violation of Bell's inequalities, ensuring the absence of local hidden variables.

• Detects eavesdropping through deviations in expected correlations.

• •

Device-Independent QKD

Device-independent QKD (DI-QKD) is a robust extension of QKD that ensures security even when the devices used are untrusted or compromised.

Key Features of DI-QKD

1. **Entanglement-Based Security:**

– Relies on the generation and measurement of entangled states.

2. **Bell Inequalities:**

– Security is guaranteed by violations of Bell inequalities, which confirm quantum behavior.

3. **Practical Applications:**

– Provides security against side-channel attacks and imperfect implementations.

• •

SECURITY PROOF OF QKD SYSTEMS

QKD's security is rooted in the laws of quantum mechanics. The following concepts are critical to understanding its robustness:

1. Quantum No-Cloning Theorem

The impossibility of copying quantum states prevents eavesdroppers (Eve) from intercepting and duplicating the transmitted photons without introducing detectable disturbances.

2. Information Disturbance Trade-off

Eve's attempt to measure quantum states disturbs them, increasing the error rate in the key. If the error rate exceeds a threshold (typically 11% for BB84), Alice and Bob can detect eavesdropping and discard the compromised key.

3. Entanglement and Bell's Theorem

In the E91 protocol, the presence of entanglement and the violation of Bell inequalities confirm the security of the key. Eavesdropping disrupts these correlations, revealing intrusion.

4. Privacy Amplification

Even if Eve gains partial information, Alice and Bob can apply privacy amplification techniques to distill a shorter, completely secure key.

Mathematical Framework

Security proofs use concepts like: $H(Key) = H(Raw\ Key) - H(Eve's\ Information)$ where H represents entropy. The goal is to minimize Eve's information to ensure the key remains secret.

PRACTICAL CONSIDERATIONS AND LIMITATIONS

Hardware Requirements

1. **Photon Sources:**

   – Single-photon sources or weak coherent pulses.

2. **Detectors:**

   – High-efficiency photon detectors are critical for accurate measurements.

3. **Quantum Channels:**

   – Fiber-optic cables or free-space optics for photon transmission.

Distance Limitations

• Signal degradation over long distances limits current QKD systems.

• Solutions:

   – **Quantum Repeaters:** Extend the range by linking intermediate nodes.

   – **Satellite-Based QKD:** Overcomes terrestrial distance limitations, demonstrated by China's Micius satellite.

Key Management

• Integration with classical systems requires robust

key management protocols to ensure usability in hybrid networks.

Cost and Scalability

- High implementation costs and technical complexity limit widespread adoption.

- Research into miniaturized and cost-effective components is ongoing.

Regulatory and Standardization Challenges

- Lack of global standards for QKD hinders interoperability and large-scale deployment.

• •

CONCLUSION

Quantum Key Distribution (QKD) is the cornerstone of quantum cryptography, offering unparalleled security through protocols like BB84 and E91. By leveraging quantum principles, such as the no-cloning theorem and entanglement, QKD ensures secure key exchange even in the presence of adversaries. While practical challenges remain, advancements in technology and infrastructure are steadily addressing these limitations, paving the way for QKD to become the backbone of secure communication in the quantum era.

CHAPTER 5: POST-QUANTUM CRYPTOGRAPHY

The advent of quantum computing poses an existential threat to classical encryption systems. Post-quantum cryptography (PQC) has emerged as a field dedicated to developing cryptographic algorithms resilient to attacks from quantum computers. This chapter explores the definition and principles of post-quantum cryptography, compares it with quantum cryptography, and delves into the primary categories of post-quantum algorithms, including lattice-based, hash-based, and code-based cryptography.

· ·

DEFINITION AND PRINCIPLES OF POST-QUANTUM CRYPTOGRAPHY

Definition

Post-quantum cryptography refers to cryptographic methods designed to resist attacks by both classical and quantum computers. Unlike quantum cryptography, which uses quantum mechanics to secure communications, PQC relies on mathematically complex problems that remain intractable even for quantum computers.

Principles of Post-Quantum Cryptography

1. **Hardness of Mathematical Problems:**

   – PQC algorithms are based on problems believed to be unsolvable by quantum algorithms like Shor's or Grover's.

   – Examples include lattice problems, structured hash functions, and error-correcting codes.

2. **Backward Compatibility:**

   – PQC is designed to integrate seamlessly with existing communication protocols, allowing for a gradual transition to quantum-resistant systems.

3. **Versatility:**

- PQC can be implemented across various devices and platforms, from high-performance servers to resource-constrained IoT devices.

4. **Long-Term Security:**

- By preempting quantum threats, PQC ensures the confidentiality of encrypted data far into the future.

. . . .

COMPARISON WITH QUANTUM CRYPTOGRAPHY

Aspect	Quantum Cryptography	Post-Quantum Cryptography
Foundation	Based on quantum mechanics	Based on hard mathematical problems
Infrastructure	Requires quantum hardware (e.g., photon sources)	Operates on classical digital infrastructure
Security Mechanism	Physical laws prevent eavesdropping	Computational hardness resists decryption
Deployment	Limited by high costs and distance constraints	Easier to integrate into existing systems
Use Cases	Key distribution	Encryption, digital signatures, authentication

While quantum cryptography offers unparalleled security, its reliance on quantum technologies limits its scalability. PQC, on the other hand, leverages existing infrastructure, making it a practical and immediate solution to quantum threats.

• •

ALGORITHMS DESIGNED FOR POST-QUANTUM RESILIENCE

Post-quantum cryptography encompasses several algorithmic approaches. The most promising categories include lattice-based, hash-based, and code-based cryptography, each with unique strengths and applications.

• •

1. Lattice-Based Cryptography

Overview

Lattice-based cryptography relies on the complexity of problems involving multi-dimensional lattices. These problems, such as the Shortest Vector Problem (SVP) and Learning with Errors (LWE), are resistant to both classical and quantum attacks.

Key Algorithms

- **NTRUEncrypt:**

    – One of the earliest lattice-based encryption schemes.

    – Combines efficiency with high security, suitable for resource-constrained devices.

- **Kyber:**

    – A secure and efficient key encapsulation mechanism (KEM) designed for PQC.

- **Dilithium:**

  – A lattice-based digital signature scheme offering strong security guarantees.

Advantages

- Highly scalable and efficient.

- Resistant to quantum attacks due to the mathematical complexity of lattice problems.

- Flexible across encryption, digital signatures, and key exchange protocols.

Applications

- Secure communication protocols like TLS (Transport Layer Security).

- Authentication systems for IoT devices.

• •

2. Hash-Based Cryptography

Overview

Hash-based cryptography relies on the security of cryptographic hash functions, such as SHA-256 or SHA-3. It is particularly suited for digital signatures, where security is derived from one-way functions.

Key Algorithms

- **Lamport Signatures:**

  – A simple one-time signature scheme using hash functions.

- **Merkle Trees:**

  – Extends Lamport signatures by organizing multiple hashes into a tree structure, enabling reusable keys.

- **SPHINCS+:**

  – A stateless, hash-based digital signature scheme providing long-term quantum resistance.

Advantages

- Strong security foundation based on well-studied hash functions.

- Minimal reliance on additional computational assumptions.

Limitations

- Larger signature sizes compared to other PQC methods.

- Primarily suited for digital signatures rather than general encryption.

• •

3. Code-Based Cryptography

Overview

Code-based cryptography is founded on the hardness of decoding random linear codes. The most prominent scheme in this category is the McEliece cryptosystem, developed in the 1970s.

Key Algorithms

- **McEliece Cryptosystem:**

    - Uses error-correcting codes to provide secure encryption.

    - Known for its robustness against quantum attacks.

- **BIKE (Bit Flipping Key Encapsulation):**

    - Combines code-based security with efficient key encapsulation.

- **HQC (Hamming Quasi-Cyclic):**

    - A hybrid approach leveraging structured codes for high efficiency.

Advantages

- Long history of security with no successful attacks to date.

- Suitable for public-key encryption and key exchange.

Limitations

- Large key sizes, which can be challenging for some applications.

- Slower than lattice-based schemes in certain scenarios.

• •

CONCLUSION

Post-quantum cryptography is a vital response to the imminent threat posed by quantum computing. By leveraging the hardness of lattice problems, the simplicity of hash functions, and the robustness of error-correcting codes, PQC provides a diverse toolkit for securing communication in the quantum era. While each approach has its strengths and limitations, their collective development ensures a resilient cryptographic future.

CHAPTER 6:
QUANTUM RANDOM NUMBER GENERATION (QRNG)

Randomness is a cornerstone of cryptographic security. From generating encryption keys to securing authentication protocols, the quality of randomness directly impacts the robustness of cryptographic systems. Quantum Random Number Generation (QRNG) represents a leap forward in randomness generation, leveraging the principles of quantum mechanics to produce numbers that are truly random. This chapter explores the importance of randomness in cryptographic systems, the mechanisms underlying QRNG, and a comparison with classical random number generators.

• •

IMPORTANCE OF RANDOMNESS IN CRYPTOGRAPHIC SYSTEMS

Cryptographic systems rely heavily on random numbers for their security and functionality.

Key Roles of Randomness

1. **Encryption Key Generation:**

   – Keys must be unpredictable to prevent adversaries from guessing or calculating them.

2. **Initialization Vectors (IVs):**

   – Used in cryptographic protocols to ensure unique encryption results, even for identical plaintexts.

3. **Salt for Hashing:**

   – Random salt values are appended to plaintext before hashing to prevent attacks like precomputed rainbow tables.

4. **Authentication Tokens:**

   – Randomness ensures secure session tokens and challenge-response protocols.

The Need for High-Quality Randomness

- **Predictability Risk:** Poor-quality randomness can make

cryptographic systems vulnerable to attacks, such as key prediction.

- **Pseudo-Randomness Limitations:** Classical generators often use deterministic algorithms, creating patterns that may be exploited.

- **True Randomness:** Only truly random numbers, generated from physical processes, can guarantee cryptographic robustness.

• •

QRNG MECHANISMS USING QUANTUM MECHANICS

Quantum Random Number Generators (QRNGs) capitalize on the inherent unpredictability of quantum phenomena to produce truly random numbers. Unlike classical systems, which rely on algorithms or physical processes susceptible to bias, QRNGs draw randomness from fundamental quantum properties.

1. Photon Detection

Photon-based QRNGs utilize the probabilistic nature of photon behavior when interacting with optical systems.

How It Works

1. **Photon Source:**

   –   A single-photon source emits photons one at a time.

2. **Beam Splitter:**

   –   The photon passes through a beam splitter, which directs it to one of two detectors with equal probability.

3. **Detection:**

   –   The detector that registers the photon assigns a binary value (e.g., 0 for one detector and 1 for the other).

Quantum Principle

The process relies on the quantum property of superposition, where the photon exists in multiple states until measured, ensuring its path is inherently random.

Advantages

- High-speed generation of random bits.

- Straightforward implementation with existing optical technology.

• •

2. Quantum Tunneling

Quantum tunneling-based QRNGs exploit the phenomenon where particles pass through potential barriers, defying classical predictions.

How It Works

1. **Tunneling Event:**

   – An electron is subjected to a potential barrier it would not cross under classical physics.

2. **Detection:**

   – The tunneling event triggers an electrical signal, which is translated into a random bit.

Quantum Principle

The occurrence of tunneling events is entirely probabilistic, determined by the wave function of the particle.

Advantages

- Compact hardware implementation using semiconductor technology.

- High throughput suitable for applications requiring massive amounts of random data.

• •

COMPARISON OF QRNG WITH CLASSICAL RANDOM NUMBER GENERATORS

Classical random number generators (RNGs) can be categorized into pseudo-random number generators (PRNGs) and true random number generators (TRNGs). While TRNGs also rely on physical processes, QRNGs surpass both in terms of randomness quality.

Pseudo-Random Number Generators (PRNGs)

- **Mechanism:**

    – Generate numbers using deterministic algorithms with an initial seed.

- **Advantages:**

    – Fast and reproducible.

    – Suitable for non-cryptographic applications.

- **Limitations:**

    – Predictable if the seed is known.

    – Patterns can emerge over long sequences.

True Random Number Generators (TRNGs)

- **Mechanism:**

  – Use physical processes like thermal noise or radioactive decay.

- **Advantages:**

  – Provides non-deterministic randomness.

- **Limitations:**

  – Susceptible to environmental influences, leading to bias or noise.

Quantum Random Number Generators (QRNGs)

- **Mechanism:**

  – Harness quantum phenomena like photon behavior or quantum tunneling.

- **Advantages:**

  – Guaranteed true randomness due to the inherent unpredictability of quantum mechanics.

  – Immune to external influences like temperature or electromagnetic noise.

- **Limitations:**

  – Higher cost and complexity compared to PRNGs and TRNGs.

Feature	PRNG	TRNG	QRNG
Randomness Quality	Pseudo-random	True random	Quantum random
Determinism	Deterministic	Non-deterministic	Non-deterministic
Susceptibility to Bias	Low with good seed	High	None
Scalability	Very high	Moderate	High
Applications	Non-critical tasks	Cryptography	High-security systems

· ·

APPLICATIONS OF QRNG

1. **Cryptographic Key Generation:**

– Ensures unbreakable encryption keys.

2. **Secure Communication:**

– Powers quantum key distribution (QKD) protocols.

3. **Scientific Simulations:**

– Provides randomness for quantum and classical simulations.

4. **Gambling and Lottery Systems:**

– Guarantees fairness and unpredictability.

• •

CONCLUSION

Quantum Random Number Generators (QRNGs) redefine randomness generation by tapping into the inherent unpredictability of quantum mechanics. Mechanisms like photon detection and quantum tunneling provide truly random outputs, surpassing the limitations of classical PRNGs and TRNGs. As QRNG technology continues to advance, its applications in cryptography and beyond promise a more secure and unpredictable future.

CHAPTER 7: BUILDING A QUANTUM KEY DISTRIBUTION NETWORK

Quantum Key Distribution (QKD) networks represent the forefront of secure communication, leveraging quantum mechanics to ensure the confidentiality and integrity of data. This chapter examines the essential components of a QKD system, the hardware requirements for implementation, and real-world use cases and existing QKD networks, including the landmark example of China's Micius satellite.

• •

COMPONENTS OF A QKD SYSTEM

A QKD system integrates quantum and classical technologies to establish a secure communication channel between two parties. The primary components include quantum channels, classical communication channels, and supporting infrastructure.

1. Quantum Channels

- **Purpose:**
  - Facilitate the transmission of quantum states, typically qubits, between the sender (Alice) and receiver (Bob).

- **Mediums:**
  - **Fiber Optic Cables:** Widely used for terrestrial QKD due to low photon loss over moderate distances.
  - **Free-Space Optics:** Employed in satellite-based QKD for long-range communication across continents or between satellites and ground stations.

- **Characteristics:**
  - Must preserve the quantum state integrity during transmission.
  - Vulnerable to environmental factors, such as scattering and attenuation, which limit transmission distances.

2. Classical Communication Channels

- **Purpose:**
  - Facilitate key reconciliation, error correction, and

eavesdropping detection between Alice and Bob.

- **Mediums:**

  – Internet or other secure classical communication systems.

- **Characteristics:**

  – While the classical channel itself need not be encrypted, it must be authenticated to prevent tampering by an adversary.

3. Key Reconciliation and Privacy Amplification

- **Key Reconciliation:**

  – Alice and Bob compare bases used during quantum state transmission to identify matching results.

  – Errors are corrected through classical error-correction protocols.

- **Privacy Amplification:**

  – Reduces any partial information an eavesdropper might have gained, ensuring a secure key.

. . . .

HARDWARE REQUIREMENTS

Implementing a QKD system requires specialized hardware to generate, manipulate, transmit, and detect quantum states.

1. Single-Photon Sources

- **Function:**

  – Emit single photons, which carry the quantum information (e.g., polarization or phase).

- **Types:**

  – **Weak Coherent Sources:** Use attenuated lasers to approximate single-photon emission.

  – **True Single-Photon Sources:** Employ quantum dots or nitrogen-vacancy centers in diamonds to generate precise single-photon states.

- **Challenges:**

  – Achieving a high emission rate while maintaining low multiphoton probabilities.

2. Quantum State Modulators

- **Function:**

  – Encode quantum information (e.g., polarization, phase) onto the photons.

- **Examples:**

  – Polarization modulators and phase modulators.

3. Photon Detectors

- **Function:**

  – Detect incoming photons at the receiver (Bob) to measure their quantum states.

- **Types:**

  – **Avalanche Photodiodes (APDs):** High sensitivity and widely used in fiber-based QKD.

  – **Superconducting Nanowire Single-Photon Detectors (SNSPDs):** Offer superior efficiency and lower dark counts, ideal for long-distance QKD.

- **Challenges:**

  – High detection efficiency and minimal noise are critical for reliable operation.

4. Quantum Repeaters

- **Purpose:**

  – Extend the range of QKD networks by mitigating signal loss and noise.

- **Mechanism:**

  – Use quantum entanglement swapping and error correction to bridge distant nodes.

- **Current Status:**

  – Still under active development; not yet widely deployed.

5. Synchronization Systems

- **Function:**

  – Ensure precise timing between Alice and Bob for accurate quantum state transmission and measurement.

- **Examples:**

  – Atomic clocks or high-precision timing circuits.

USE CASES AND EXISTING QKD NETWORKS

QKD networks are being deployed in diverse applications, from securing military communications to enabling privacy in financial transactions. Let's explore some key use cases and prominent implementations.

1. Use Cases

- **Military and Government Communications:**

    - Secure exchange of classified information and operational commands.

- **Financial Institutions:**

    - Protects transactions and prevents fraud in banking systems.

- **Healthcare:**

    - Ensures patient data confidentiality during transfers between hospitals and research institutions.

- **Critical Infrastructure:**

    - Secures control systems in energy grids, water supplies, and transportation.

2. Existing QKD Networks

China's Micius Satellite

- **Overview:**

- – Launched in 2016, Micius is the world's first quantum communication satellite.

- **Features:**

  - – Facilitates satellite-to-ground QKD over distances exceeding 1,200 kilometers.

  - – Demonstrated secure key exchange between China and Europe.

  - – Combined QKD with classical encryption to send quantum-secured emails.

- **Significance:**

  - – Established the feasibility of global quantum-secure communication.

Quantum Network in Europe (Quantum Internet Alliance)

- **Overview:**

  - – A consortium of research institutions developing a pan-European quantum communication network.

- **Goals:**

  - – Integrate QKD into existing communication infrastructure.

  - – Enable long-distance quantum communication through entanglement-based protocols.

Tokyo QKD Network

- **Overview:**

  - – A metropolitan QKD network deployed in Tokyo, Japan.

- **Features:**

  - – Connects multiple institutions, including government agencies, banks, and universities.

  - – Uses a hybrid approach combining fiber optics and satellite links.

DARPA Quantum Network (USA)

- **Overview:**

  - One of the earliest QKD networks, developed by the U.S. Department of Defense.

- **Features:**

  - Established secure links between military bases and research facilities.

  - Pioneered research into scalable quantum communication systems.

• •

CHALLENGES IN BUILDING QKD NETWORKS

While QKD networks hold immense promise, several challenges must be addressed for widespread deployment:

1. **Cost:**

   – High initial investment in specialized hardware and infrastructure.

2. **Distance Limitations:**

   – Signal loss in fiber-optic cables and atmospheric interference in free-space optics limit range.

3. **Integration with Classical Systems:**

   – Ensuring compatibility with existing communication protocols and infrastructure.

4. **Standardization:**

   – Lack of global standards for QKD implementation and interoperability.

• •

CONCLUSION

Building a QKD network requires integrating quantum channels, classical communication channels, and sophisticated hardware like single-photon sources and detectors. Use cases for QKD span critical industries, ensuring secure communication in applications ranging from national defense to financial transactions. Existing networks, such as China's Micius satellite and Europe's quantum internet initiatives, demonstrate the feasibility of scaling QKD to global levels. Despite challenges, advancements in technology and infrastructure continue to pave the way for a secure quantum communication future.

CHAPTER 8: SECURING COMMUNICATIONS WITH QUANTUM ENCRYPTION

Quantum encryption represents a transformative leap in secure communication, ensuring confidentiality, integrity, and authenticity in a world increasingly vulnerable to cyber threats. This chapter examines the practical implementation of quantum encryption in secure messaging systems and virtual private networks (VPNs). Additionally, it explores protocols for integrating Quantum Key Distribution (QKD) with classical encryption to achieve hybrid, quantum-secure communication systems.

• •

IMPLEMENTATION OF QUANTUM ENCRYPTION IN SECURE MESSAGING SYSTEMS

Secure messaging systems are essential for safeguarding sensitive information in personal and professional communications. The integration of quantum encryption elevates these systems to an unprecedented level of security.

1. Overview of Secure Messaging with Quantum Encryption

Quantum encryption secures messaging systems by replacing or enhancing traditional encryption algorithms with keys generated through QKD. These quantum-derived keys are inherently resistant to brute-force attacks and eavesdropping.

2. Architecture of a Quantum-Encrypted Messaging System

1. **Key Exchange:**

   – QKD is used to establish a secure session key between the sender and recipient.

2. **Message Encryption:**

   – The session key encrypts the message using a classical encryption algorithm (e.g., AES-256).

3. **Message Transmission:**

- The encrypted message is transmitted over a classical network.

4. **Message Decryption:**

- The recipient uses the shared session key to decrypt the message.

3. Features and Benefits

- **Unbreakable Key Security:**

  - The keys generated through QKD are immune to quantum computing attacks.

- **Eavesdropping Detection:**

  - Any attempt to intercept the QKD process introduces detectable errors.

- **Scalability:**

  - Can be integrated into existing messaging platforms, such as Signal or WhatsApp, with minor modifications.

4. Challenges

- **Latency:**

  - The QKD process introduces additional communication overhead.

- **Hardware Dependency:**

  - Requires specialized equipment like single-photon detectors, which may not be practical for consumer-grade devices.

Case Study: Quantum-Encrypted Messaging Prototype

A prototype quantum-encrypted messaging application was successfully demonstrated between two research institutions using a fiber-optic QKD network. The system achieved real-time encryption and decryption, showcasing the feasibility of implementing quantum encryption in practical messaging systems.

IMPLEMENTATION OF QUANTUM ENCRYPTION IN VIRTUAL PRIVATE NETWORKS (VPNS)

VPNs are widely used to establish secure connections over public networks. Quantum encryption enhances VPNs by securing the key exchange process and ensuring the confidentiality of transmitted data.

1. Quantum-Encrypted VPN Architecture

1. **Key Distribution:**

   – The VPN server and client use QKD to exchange a session key.

2. **Data Encryption:**

   – The session key encrypts the VPN tunnel using a symmetric encryption algorithm.

3. **Authentication:**

   – Device-independent QKD ensures secure authentication by verifying the integrity of the quantum channel.

2. Quantum Encryption Protocol for VPNs

- **Hybrid Protocols:**

  – Combine QKD with traditional VPN protocols like OpenVPN or IPsec to create a hybrid quantum-encrypted VPN.

- **Dynamic Key Refreshing:**

  – Periodically refreshes encryption keys using QKD to maintain security against long-term attacks.

3. Features and Benefits

- **Quantum-Resilient Security:**

  – Prevents attackers from decrypting VPN traffic even with future quantum computers.

- **Continuous Authentication:**

  – Detects any attempt to tamper with the quantum channel or session key.

- **Adaptability:**

  – Supports integration with existing VPN infrastructure.

4. Challenges

- **Cost:**

  – The deployment of quantum encryption hardware increases initial setup costs.

- **Distance Limitations:**

  – Fiber-based QKD in VPNs is limited to metropolitan or regional networks without quantum repeaters.

Case Study: Quantum-Enhanced Corporate VPN

A multinational corporation deployed a quantum-encrypted VPN to secure communications between its headquarters and regional offices. Using a fiber-optic QKD network, the system achieved low-latency and high-security communication.

• •

PROTOCOLS FOR INTEGRATING QKD WITH CLASSICAL ENCRYPTION

Hybrid systems that integrate QKD with classical encryption leverage the strengths of both approaches, providing practical and robust solutions for secure communication.

1. Hybrid Encryption Framework

A hybrid encryption system uses QKD to generate secure session keys while employing classical encryption for data transmission. This approach allows seamless integration into existing infrastructure.

Steps in a Hybrid Protocol

1. **Key Distribution:**

   – Use QKD to generate and share a session key between two parties.

2. **Data Encryption:**

   – Encrypt data with the session key using classical encryption (e.g., AES-256 or ChaCha20).

3. **Key Management:**

   – Periodically update the session key through QKD to ensure forward security.

2. TLS with QKD Integration

Transport Layer Security (TLS) is the standard protocol for securing web communications. QKD can be integrated into TLS to enhance its security.

Modified TLS Workflow

1. **Key Exchange:**

   – Replace RSA or Diffie-Hellman key exchange with QKD.

2. **Encryption:**

   – Use the QKD-derived key for session encryption.

3. **Authentication:**

   – Authenticate the quantum channel using digital certificates or quantum-secured signatures.

Benefits of QKD-Enhanced TLS

• **Quantum-Safe Handshake:**

   – Eliminates vulnerabilities in traditional key exchange algorithms.

• **Backward Compatibility:**

   – Retains compatibility with existing TLS frameworks while adding quantum security.

3. Challenges in QKD Integration

1. **Latency and Throughput:**

   – QKD adds additional steps to the handshake process, potentially increasing latency.

2. **Infrastructure Requirements:**

   – Requires QKD hardware for end-to-end implementation, which may not be practical for all use cases.

3. **Standardization:**

   – The lack of standardized protocols for QKD integration poses interoperability challenges.

CONCLUSION

Quantum encryption has the potential to revolutionize secure communication by enhancing messaging systems, VPNs, and other secure channels. Through the integration of QKD with classical encryption protocols, hybrid systems offer a practical and scalable path to achieving quantum-resilient security. While challenges such as cost and infrastructure limitations remain, ongoing advancements in quantum technology and standardization efforts are bringing these solutions closer to widespread adoption.

CHAPTER 9: QUANTUM-SECURE CLOUD STORAGE

Cloud storage has become an integral part of modern computing, enabling businesses and individuals to store and access data remotely. However, the rise of cyberattacks and the impending threat of quantum computers make traditional encryption methods inadequate for long-term data protection. Quantum encryption, specifically through Quantum Key Distribution (QKD), offers a solution for ensuring secure, end-to-end encryption in cloud storage. This chapter presents a comprehensive framework for applying quantum encryption to cloud services, explores the mechanisms for ensuring end-to-end encryption with QKD, and addresses the challenges of scalability and cost-effectiveness.

• •

FRAMEWORK FOR APPLYING QUANTUM ENCRYPTION IN CLOUD SERVICES

To secure cloud storage using quantum encryption, a well-defined framework must integrate quantum technologies with existing cloud infrastructure. The framework involves several key components and steps.

1. Architecture of Quantum-Secure Cloud Storage

1. **Data Encryption:**

   – Data is encrypted on the client side using a symmetric encryption algorithm (e.g., AES-256).

2. **Quantum Key Exchange:**

   – QKD is used to securely exchange encryption keys between the client and the cloud provider.

3. **Secure Storage:**

   – Encrypted data is stored on cloud servers, ensuring that unauthorized access does not compromise the plaintext data.

4. **Key Management:**

   – Encryption keys are managed securely using quantum-safe mechanisms, with periodic key updates via QKD.

2. Steps for Implementing Quantum-Secure Cloud Storage

1. **Client-Side Encryption:**

   – Data is encrypted before it is uploaded to the cloud, ensuring confidentiality even if the server is breached.

2. **Integration of QKD:**

   – A QKD link is established between the client and the cloud provider to securely exchange encryption keys.

3. **Authentication:**

   – Digital signatures or quantum-secured authentication mechanisms are used to verify the identity of both parties.

4. **Data Retrieval:**

   – The client retrieves encrypted data, decrypting it locally using the QKD-derived key.

3. Features of the Framework

- **End-to-End Encryption:**

   – Data remains encrypted throughout its lifecycle, from storage to retrieval.

- **Eavesdropping Detection:**

   – Any interception attempt during the QKD process introduces detectable errors.

- **Quantum-Safe Security:**

   – Keys exchanged through QKD are immune to quantum computing attacks.

• •

ENSURING END-TO-END ENCRYPTION WITH QKD

End-to-end encryption ensures that data remains protected throughout its journey, from the client to the cloud and back. QKD plays a pivotal role in establishing a secure channel for key exchange, enabling robust encryption.

1. Key Distribution with QKD

1. **Initialization:**

   – The client and cloud provider initialize a QKD session.

2. **Key Exchange:**

   – QKD generates a shared secret key through the secure transmission of quantum states.

3. **Key Verification:**

   – Both parties verify the key's integrity through error-checking protocols.

4. **Encryption Key Derivation:**

   – The shared secret is used to derive encryption keys for securing data.

2. Hybrid Encryption

To achieve quantum-secure end-to-end encryption, a hybrid approach is often used:

• **Symmetric Encryption for Data:**

– Data is encrypted using a classical symmetric algorithm (e.g., AES-256) for speed and efficiency.

- **QKD for Key Exchange:**

– The encryption keys are exchanged securely using QKD, ensuring resistance to quantum attacks.

3. Integration with Cloud Platforms

1. **Quantum-Secure API:**

– Cloud providers offer APIs that support QKD-based key exchange for seamless integration with client applications.

2. **Hardware Integration:**

– Quantum encryption hardware (e.g., photon detectors) is deployed at cloud data centers to support QKD.

3. **Audit Trails:**

– Secure logging mechanisms track key exchanges and data access, ensuring accountability.

4. Advantages of End-to-End Encryption with QKD

- **Uncompromised Security:**

– Even if the cloud server is breached, encrypted data remains inaccessible without the QKD-derived keys.

- **Future-Proofing:**

– Provides long-term protection against quantum and classical attacks.

• •

CHALLENGES IN SCALABILITY AND COST-EFFECTIVENESS

While quantum encryption offers unmatched security, its implementation in cloud storage systems faces significant challenges related to scalability and cost.

1. Scalability Challenges

1. **Infrastructure Requirements:**

    –   QKD relies on specialized hardware, such as single-photon sources and detectors, which are not widely available.

2. **Distance Limitations:**

    –   Fiber-optic QKD is limited to distances of a few hundred kilometers without the use of quantum repeaters, making it unsuitable for global-scale applications.

3. **Integration Complexity:**

    –   Incorporating QKD into existing cloud platforms requires significant modifications to both hardware and software infrastructure.

2. Cost Challenges

1. **High Initial Investment:**

    –   The cost of quantum hardware and the deployment of QKD networks is prohibitively high for most organizations.

2. **Maintenance Costs:**

– Maintaining and upgrading quantum hardware adds to the overall expense.

3. **User Costs:**

– Cloud providers may pass the additional costs of quantum encryption to users, limiting adoption.

3. Potential Solutions

1. **Hybrid Deployment:**

– Use QKD for high-priority data while relying on classical encryption for less sensitive information to optimize costs.

2. **Quantum Repeaters:**

– Develop and deploy quantum repeaters to extend the range of QKD networks, reducing the need for redundant infrastructure.

3. **Economies of Scale:**

– Large-scale adoption of quantum technologies can drive down costs over time through mass production and standardization.

• •

REAL-WORLD APPLICATIONS AND EXAMPLES

1. **Government Data Protection:**

- Governments can use quantum-secure cloud storage to protect classified information and citizen data.

2. **Financial Services:**

- Banks and financial institutions can safeguard transaction records and customer information against cyberattacks.

3. **Healthcare:**

- Securely store and share patient data among healthcare providers, ensuring compliance with privacy regulations.

. . . .

CONCLUSION

Quantum-secure cloud storage represents the next frontier in data security, offering unparalleled protection against both classical and quantum threats. By integrating QKD into cloud services, organizations can ensure end-to-end encryption for sensitive data. However, challenges related to scalability and cost-effectiveness must be addressed to achieve widespread adoption. With continued advancements in quantum technology and infrastructure, quantum-secure cloud storage is poised to become a standard for securing data in the digital age.

CHAPTER 10: QUANTUM BLOCKCHAIN AND DECENTRALIZED SYSTEMS

Blockchain technology, the foundation of decentralized systems, has transformed industries like finance, supply chain, and identity management. However, the emergence of quantum computing presents a potential threat to blockchain's cryptographic foundations. By integrating quantum encryption and developing quantum-resistant consensus mechanisms, blockchain technology can remain secure in the quantum era. This chapter explores how quantum encryption can be integrated into blockchain systems, examines quantum-resistant consensus mechanisms, and discusses applications in decentralized finance (DeFi) and identity management.

• •

INTEGRATION OF QUANTUM ENCRYPTION INTO BLOCKCHAIN TECHNOLOGY

Blockchain relies on cryptographic techniques to ensure security, data integrity, and immutability. Quantum encryption enhances these properties, providing a defense against quantum computing threats.

1. Blockchain's Cryptographic Vulnerabilities

1. **Digital Signatures:**

    –   Public-key cryptography (e.g., RSA, ECDSA) secures digital signatures in blockchain systems.

    –   Vulnerable to quantum algorithms like Shor's algorithm, which can efficiently break these cryptographic schemes.

2. **Hashing Algorithms:**

    –   Hash functions like SHA-256 ensure data integrity.

    –   While resistant to quantum attacks, Grover's algorithm can halve their effective security level.

2. Quantum Encryption for Securing Blockchain

1. **Quantum Key Distribution (QKD):**

– Provides quantum-secure communication channels for node-to-node communication in blockchain networks.

2. **Post-Quantum Cryptography (PQC):**

– Integrates quantum-resistant cryptographic algorithms (e.g., lattice-based cryptography) into blockchain protocols.

3. **Quantum-Safe Digital Signatures:**

– Replaces vulnerable ECDSA and RSA signatures with quantum-secure alternatives like Dilithium or SPHINCS +.

3. Implementation in Blockchain Architecture

1. **Smart Contract Security:**

– Smart contracts use quantum-secure keys for authentication and execution, ensuring resistance to tampering.

2. **Inter-Node Communication:**

– Nodes in the blockchain network communicate using QKD-secured channels, preventing eavesdropping or man-in-the-middle attacks.

3. **Key Management:**

– Quantum-secure key management systems prevent the exposure of private keys, even in the event of quantum-based attacks.

4. Benefits of Quantum Encryption in Blockchain

• **Future-Proof Security:**

– Ensures that blockchain systems remain secure against current and future threats.

• **Enhanced Privacy:**

   –   Quantum encryption strengthens privacy in public and permissioned blockchain networks.

- **Scalability:**

   –   Facilitates the development of scalable blockchain solutions that are resistant to computational advancements.

• •

QUANTUM-RESISTANT CONSENSUS MECHANISMS

Consensus mechanisms are critical to blockchain networks, ensuring agreement among nodes on the validity of transactions. Quantum computing challenges traditional consensus mechanisms, necessitating the development of quantum-resistant alternatives.

1. Vulnerabilities in Classical Consensus Mechanisms

1. **Proof of Work (PoW):**

    – Mining relies on solving computationally intensive puzzles.

    – Quantum computers can use Grover's algorithm to perform this work more efficiently, potentially destabilizing the network.

2. **Proof of Stake (PoS):**

    – Relies on cryptographic keys for staking and voting.

    – Vulnerable to quantum attacks on key-based systems.

2. Quantum-Resistant Consensus Models

1. **Post-Quantum Proof of Work (PQ-PoW):**

    – Uses hash functions that are resistant to quantum

attacks (e.g., SHA-3 variants).

–   Ensures computational fairness in mining, even with quantum capabilities.

2. **Proof of Entanglement (PoE):**

–   Leverages quantum entanglement to validate blocks.

–   Nodes use quantum states to demonstrate their commitment to the network.

3. **Hybrid Consensus Mechanisms:**

–   Combines quantum-resistant PoW with quantum-secure PoS to balance energy efficiency and security.

3. Benefits of Quantum-Resistant Consensus

•   **Security:**

–   Prevents quantum-capable adversaries from monopolizing the network.

•   **Sustainability:**

–   Reduces energy consumption through more efficient consensus mechanisms.

•   **Trust:**

–   Enhances trust in blockchain systems by ensuring resilience against emerging threats.

• •

APPLICATIONS IN DECENTRALIZED FINANCE (DEFI) AND IDENTITY MANAGEMENT

Quantum encryption and blockchain technology together unlock new possibilities for secure and efficient decentralized systems.

1. Decentralized Finance (DeFi)

Quantum encryption strengthens the security of DeFi platforms, which manage sensitive financial transactions and assets.

Key Applications

1. **Secure Smart Contracts:**

   – Quantum-encrypted keys ensure the integrity of smart contracts governing DeFi transactions.

2. **Quantum-Safe Token Transfers:**

   – Quantum-secure wallets protect cryptocurrency transactions from interception or fraud.

3. **Enhanced Privacy:**

   – Quantum encryption enables privacy-preserving DeFi protocols, ensuring user anonymity while maintaining compliance with regulations.

Case Study: Quantum-Resilient DeFi Protocol

A pilot project demonstrated the integration of quantum encryption into a DeFi lending platform, ensuring secure transactions and quantum-safe asset management.

• •

2. Identity Management

Identity management systems leverage blockchain for decentralized and tamper-proof records. Quantum encryption ensures the security of sensitive identity data.

Key Applications

1. **Self-Sovereign Identity (SSI):**

   –   Users control their digital identities, secured by quantum encryption.

2. **Secure Biometric Authentication:**

   –   Quantum-secure keys protect biometric data used in identity verification.

3. **Cross-Border Identity Verification:**

   –   Blockchain-based quantum encryption facilitates secure and efficient cross-border identity validation.

Case Study: Quantum-Encrypted Identity System

A government-led initiative used quantum encryption in a blockchain-based identity management system, ensuring secure access to healthcare and social services.

• •

CHALLENGES AND FUTURE DIRECTIONS

Challenges

1. **Infrastructure Requirements:**

   – Implementing quantum encryption requires significant investments in hardware and software.

2. **Standardization:**

   – Lack of standardized protocols for quantum blockchain systems hinders interoperability.

3. **Scalability:**

   – Combining quantum encryption with blockchain scalability remains a technical challenge.

Future Directions

1. **Development of Quantum-Resistant Algorithms:**

   – Continued innovation in PQC and QKD will strengthen blockchain security.

2. **Global Collaboration:**

   – International standards for quantum-secure blockchain systems will drive adoption.

3. **Integration with Quantum Computing:**

   – Leveraging quantum computing for blockchain optimization while ensuring security.

· ·

CONCLUSION

Quantum encryption and blockchain technology are a natural pairing, offering enhanced security and resilience against future threats. By integrating quantum encryption into blockchain systems, developing quantum-resistant consensus mechanisms, and applying these innovations to DeFi and identity management, we can ensure the continued growth and security of decentralized systems. As quantum and blockchain technologies evolve, their convergence promises to redefine the future of secure and decentralized systems.

CHAPTER 11: HYBRID ENCRYPTION FRAMEWORKS

As quantum computing advances, organizations face the challenge of transitioning from classical encryption to quantum-safe methods. Hybrid encryption frameworks offer a practical solution by combining classical and quantum encryption techniques. This chapter explores the concept of hybrid encryption, outlines how to design systems for a gradual transition to quantum-safe encryption, and presents case studies on the implementation of hybrid frameworks in various industries.

. . . .

COMBINING CLASSICAL AND QUANTUM ENCRYPTION METHODS

Hybrid encryption frameworks integrate classical encryption with quantum technologies, leveraging the strengths of both to achieve secure and scalable systems.

1. Rationale for Hybrid Encryption

1. **Compatibility:**

   – Ensures interoperability with existing infrastructure while introducing quantum-safe elements.

2. **Future-Proofing:**

   – Incorporates quantum encryption to address threats posed by quantum computing.

3. **Scalability:**

   – Combines the efficiency of classical encryption with the robustness of quantum techniques.

2. Architecture of Hybrid Encryption Frameworks

1. **Classical Encryption Layer:**

   – Uses symmetric algorithms like AES-256 for data

encryption due to their speed and efficiency.

2. **Quantum Encryption Layer:**

– Employs Quantum Key Distribution (QKD) for secure key exchange.

3. **Key Management:**

– Combines quantum-safe methods (e.g., lattice-based cryptography) with traditional approaches for key storage and renewal.

4. **Authentication:**

– Uses quantum-resistant digital signatures (e.g., Dilithium, SPHINCS+) for verifying identities.

3. Communication Flow in Hybrid Systems

1. **Key Exchange:**

– QKD generates and shares encryption keys over a secure quantum channel.

2. **Data Encryption:**

– Classical algorithms encrypt the data using the keys obtained from QKD.

3. **Transmission:**

– Encrypted data is transmitted over a classical communication network.

4. **Decryption:**

– The recipient uses the QKD-derived key to decrypt the data.

4. Benefits of Hybrid Encryption

• **Enhanced Security:**

– Combines the resilience of quantum encryption with the efficiency of classical encryption.

- **Gradual Transition:**

  – Allows organizations to adopt quantum-safe practices incrementally.

- **Cost-Effective:**

  – Optimizes resource use by deploying quantum technologies where they are most needed.

• •

DESIGNING HYBRID SYSTEMS FOR GRADUAL TRANSITION TO QUANTUM-SAFE ENCRYPTION

A structured approach is essential for organizations looking to implement hybrid encryption systems.

1. Assessment of Current Systems

1. **Vulnerability Analysis:**

   – Identify components susceptible to quantum attacks, such as RSA and ECDSA-based systems.

2. **Critical Data Identification:**

   – Determine which data and processes require immediate quantum-safe protection.

2. Phased Implementation Strategy

1. **Pilot Projects:**

   – Begin with small-scale deployments to test hybrid encryption's effectiveness and compatibility.

2. **Incremental Integration:**

- Gradually integrate QKD and quantum-safe algorithms into existing systems.

3. **Key Updates:**

- Transition to quantum-resistant key management while retaining classical encryption for data operations.

4. **Full Migration:**

- Replace vulnerable classical components with quantum-safe alternatives once infrastructure and standards are fully developed.

3. Key Design Principles

1. **Modularity:**

- Build systems that allow independent updates to classical and quantum components.

2. **Interoperability:**

- Ensure compatibility with existing protocols and hardware.

3. **Performance Optimization:**

- Balance security with speed and efficiency by leveraging the strengths of classical algorithms for data encryption and quantum methods for key exchange.

4. Risk Management

1. **Backward Compatibility:**

- Maintain support for legacy systems during the transition period.

2. **Compliance:**

- Adhere to emerging standards for quantum-safe cryptography from organizations like NIST and ETSI.

• •

CASE STUDIES ON HYBRID FRAMEWORKS IN INDUSTRIES

The adoption of hybrid encryption frameworks is gaining momentum across industries. These case studies highlight successful implementations and their benefits.

1. Financial Services

- **Scenario:**
  - A global bank implemented a hybrid encryption framework to secure interbank transactions and customer data.

- **Implementation:**
  - QKD was deployed for key exchange between regional data centers, while AES-256 was used for encrypting transaction data.

- **Benefits:**
  - Enhanced security against future quantum threats.
  - Seamless integration with existing financial infrastructure.

- **Challenges:**
  - High initial cost for QKD hardware deployment.

• •

2. Healthcare

- **Scenario:**

  – A hospital network adopted hybrid encryption to secure patient data shared between facilities.

- **Implementation:**

  – QKD was used to exchange keys for encrypting patient records, with SHA-3 for data integrity checks.

- **Benefits:**

  – Compliance with privacy regulations (e.g., GDPR, HIPAA).

  – Improved resilience to cyberattacks.

- **Challenges:**

  – Limited availability of quantum-secure authentication systems.

• •

3. Government Communications

- **Scenario:**

  – A government agency integrated hybrid encryption to protect classified communications.

- **Implementation:**

  – Satellite-based QKD enabled secure key distribution, while traditional protocols like TLS were enhanced with quantum-resistant algorithms.

- **Benefits:**

  – Future-proof security for sensitive data.

  – Enhanced trust in diplomatic communications.

- **Challenges:**

    –   Technical complexity in combining quantum and classical systems.

• •

4. Supply Chain Management

- **Scenario:**

  –   A multinational corporation used hybrid encryption to secure its supply chain data.

- **Implementation:**

  –   Quantum encryption protected data shared between suppliers, while blockchain technology ensured transparency.

- **Benefits:**

  –   Increased data integrity and confidentiality.

  –   Streamlined compliance with international trade regulations.

- **Challenges:**

  –   Integration issues with legacy supply chain software.

• •

CHALLENGES AND FUTURE DIRECTIONS

Challenges

1. **Cost of Implementation:**

   – Quantum hardware, such as QKD systems, is expensive and may not be accessible to small businesses.

2. **Scalability:**

   – Adapting hybrid frameworks for global or large-scale operations is challenging due to the range limitations of QKD.

3. **Standardization:**

   – Lack of uniform standards for hybrid encryption systems hinders interoperability.

Future Directions

1. **Advancements in Quantum Hardware:**

   – Miniaturization and cost reduction in quantum devices will accelerate adoption.

2. **Development of Standards:**

   – Organizations like ISO and NIST are working toward standardizing hybrid encryption protocols.

3. **Integration with Emerging Technologies:**

   – Combining hybrid encryption with AI and blockchain will unlock new applications in secure communication and data processing.

. . . .

CONCLUSION

Hybrid encryption frameworks bridge the gap between classical and quantum encryption, offering a practical pathway to quantum-safe security. By combining the strengths of both approaches, these frameworks provide enhanced security, compatibility, and scalability. Through phased implementation and adherence to key design principles, industries such as finance, healthcare, government, and supply chain management are already demonstrating the potential of hybrid encryption to secure the future of data and communication.

CHAPTER 12: QUANTUM ENCRYPTION IN IOT SYSTEMS

The Internet of Things (IoT) connects billions of devices worldwide, from home appliances to industrial sensors. However, the rapid growth of IoT ecosystems has brought significant security challenges. These challenges are compounded by the potential of quantum computers to break traditional encryption, necessitating the adoption of quantum encryption methods. This chapter examines the unique challenges of securing IoT devices, presents a framework for implementing lightweight quantum encryption, and explores practical solutions tailored to the needs of IoT ecosystems.

• •

CHALLENGES OF SECURING IOT DEVICES

IoT devices are inherently vulnerable due to their limited resources, diverse architectures, and deployment in often unsecured environments. The introduction of quantum computing exacerbates these vulnerabilities, making traditional security methods insufficient.

1. Resource Constraints

- **Limited Processing Power:**

    – Many IoT devices have minimal computational capabilities, making it challenging to implement resource-intensive encryption algorithms.

- **Low Memory:**

    – Storage limitations restrict the ability to maintain large cryptographic keys or certificates.

- **Battery Life:**

    – Power efficiency is critical, and cryptographic operations can drain energy resources.

2. Scalability

- **Massive Device Numbers:**

    – IoT ecosystems often involve thousands or millions of devices, requiring scalable security solutions.

- **Heterogeneous Devices:**

  – IoT networks consist of devices with varied capabilities and manufacturers, complicating standardization.

3. Physical and Network Vulnerabilities

- **Unsecured Deployment:**

  – IoT devices are frequently installed in remote or public locations, making them susceptible to physical tampering.

- **Weak Authentication:**

  – Default passwords or lack of robust authentication methods leave devices open to attacks.

- **Man-in-the-Middle Attacks:**

  – Communication between devices is often unsecured, making it vulnerable to interception or tampering.

4. Quantum Threat

- **Breakdown of Classical Cryptography:**

  – Algorithms like RSA and ECC, commonly used in IoT, are vulnerable to quantum attacks, requiring immediate migration to quantum-safe alternatives.

• •

FRAMEWORK FOR IMPLEMENTING LIGHTWEIGHT QUANTUM ENCRYPTION

To secure IoT ecosystems against both classical and quantum threats, a lightweight quantum encryption framework is essential. This framework addresses the constraints and scalability requirements of IoT devices while leveraging quantum-safe technologies.

1. Key Components of the Framework

1. **Quantum-Safe Algorithms:**

   – Lightweight cryptographic algorithms, such as lattice-based encryption, are designed for devices with limited resources.

   – Example: NTRUEncrypt, a lattice-based algorithm suitable for constrained environments.

2. **Quantum Key Distribution (QKD):**

   – QKD is implemented between IoT gateways and cloud servers to secure communication channels.

3. **Authentication Mechanisms:**

   – Quantum-resistant digital signatures, such as

Dilithium or SPHINCS+, ensure device authentication.

4. **Efficient Key Management:**

– Centralized or decentralized quantum-safe key management systems handle the secure distribution and renewal of encryption keys.

2. Steps for Implementation

1. **Assessment of Device Capabilities:**

– Evaluate the computational, memory, and energy constraints of IoT devices to select appropriate cryptographic methods.

2. **Integration of Lightweight Cryptography:**

– Implement quantum-safe algorithms optimized for low-resource devices.

3. **Secure Communication Protocols:**

– Adopt secure IoT communication protocols, such as MQTT or CoAP, enhanced with quantum encryption.

4. **Authentication and Access Control:**

– Deploy lightweight authentication systems using quantum-resistant keys or signatures.

5. **Periodic Key Updates:**

– Use QKD or post-quantum key exchange protocols to refresh encryption keys regularly.

3. Architectural Considerations

1. **Edge-to-Cloud Security:**

– Ensure that data is encrypted from the device level (edge) to the cloud, maintaining end-to-end security.

2. **Hybrid Encryption:**

– Combine classical encryption for data transmission with quantum-safe methods for key exchange to balance security and efficiency.

3. **Quantum-Ready Gateways:**

–   Use IoT gateways equipped with quantum-safe hardware to manage communication between devices and the cloud.

• •

PRACTICAL SOLUTIONS FOR IOT ECOSYSTEMS

The following practical solutions address the challenges and implement the framework for quantum-secure IoT systems.

1. Lightweight Quantum-Safe Algorithms

- **Examples:**

  - **NTRUEncrypt:**

    - Efficient lattice-based encryption suitable for IoT devices.

  - **Saber:**

    - Lightweight post-quantum key exchange algorithm.

- **Advantages:**

  - Reduced computational and memory requirements.

  - Scalability for large IoT networks.

2. Secure Firmware Updates

- **Quantum-Safe Signatures:**

  - Use quantum-resistant digital signatures to validate firmware updates, ensuring integrity and authenticity.

- **Over-the-Air (OTA) Updates:**

  - Secure OTA mechanisms with quantum-encrypted

communication channels.

3. Authentication and Identity Management

- **Quantum-Resistant Certificates:**

  – Deploy certificates using post-quantum algorithms for secure device authentication.

- **Decentralized Identity (DID):**

  – Use blockchain-based quantum-secure identity systems to manage device credentials.

4. Communication Protocols

- **Enhanced MQTT:**

  – Integrate quantum encryption into MQTT, a lightweight protocol for IoT communication.

- **Secure CoAP:**

  – Implement quantum-safe encryption for the Constrained Application Protocol (CoAP) used in resource-limited environments.

5. IoT Gateway Security

- **Quantum-Safe Gateways:**

  – Gateways act as intermediaries, applying quantum encryption for communication between IoT devices and the cloud.

- **Key Aggregation:**

  – Use gateways to manage and distribute quantum-safe keys to connected devices.

6. AI-Driven Security

- **Anomaly Detection:**

  – Combine AI with quantum-safe cryptography to identify and respond to potential security threats in real-time.

- **Predictive Maintenance:**

  – Secure AI-driven IoT analytics with quantum encryption to prevent tampering or data breaches.

• •

CASE STUDIES

1. Smart Cities

- **Scenario:**

  - A smart city deployed quantum-encrypted IoT systems to secure data from sensors monitoring traffic, utilities, and public safety.

- **Implementation:**

  - Lightweight lattice-based encryption protected sensor communication, while QKD secured inter-gateway communication.

- **Benefits:**

  - Enhanced data integrity and real-time anomaly detection.

2. Healthcare IoT

- **Scenario:**

  - A hospital used quantum-safe IoT devices to monitor patients remotely.

- **Implementation:**

  - Secure firmware updates and communication channels ensured patient privacy and regulatory compliance.

- **Benefits:**

  - Protected sensitive medical data against quantum threats.

3. Industrial IoT (IIoT)

- **Scenario:**

  - An industrial plant integrated quantum encryption to secure IoT devices controlling machinery and monitoring production.

- **Implementation:**

  - Quantum-safe authentication mechanisms ensured that only authorized devices accessed critical systems.

- **Benefits:**

  - Prevented sabotage and ensured operational continuity.

• •

CHALLENGES AND FUTURE DIRECTIONS

Challenges

1. **Cost of Implementation:**

   – Quantum encryption hardware may be expensive for large-scale IoT deployments.

2. **Standardization:**

   – Lack of standardized quantum-safe protocols for IoT complicates implementation.

3. **Scalability:**

   – Ensuring security in massive IoT networks without sacrificing performance is a significant challenge.

Future Directions

1. **Miniaturization of Quantum Hardware:**

   – Advances in quantum hardware will make lightweight devices feasible for IoT applications.

2. **Standardization Efforts:**

   – Organizations like ETSI and NIST are working on standards for post-quantum cryptography in IoT.

3. **Integration with Emerging Technologies:**

   – Combining IoT with blockchain and AI secured by quantum encryption will create robust, intelligent ecosystems.

CONCLUSION

Quantum encryption offers transformative potential for securing IoT systems against current and future threats. By addressing resource constraints, scalability, and integration challenges, lightweight quantum encryption frameworks can be effectively deployed across diverse IoT ecosystems. As the IoT landscape continues to grow, the adoption of quantum encryption will be essential for building secure, resilient, and future-ready systems.

CHAPTER 13: QUANTUM ENCRYPTION IN MILITARY AND GOVERNMENT APPLICATIONS

The security of military and government communications is paramount, as these domains handle sensitive information critical to national defense, diplomacy, and public safety. Quantum encryption offers unparalleled protection, ensuring that even the most advanced adversaries cannot compromise communications. This chapter explores the high-security applications of quantum encryption in military and government settings, quantum-resistant frameworks for national defense, and the ethical and geopolitical implications of this transformative technology.

• •

HIGH-SECURITY APPLICATIONS OF QUANTUM ENCRYPTION

Military and government operations require secure channels for communication, intelligence sharing, and critical infrastructure protection. Quantum encryption addresses these needs by leveraging the principles of quantum mechanics to achieve unbreakable security.

1. Secure Communications

Quantum encryption ensures that communications between military and government entities remain confidential and tamper-proof.

1. **Command and Control Systems:**

   – Quantum Key Distribution (QKD) secures communication between command centers and deployed units, preventing interception or manipulation.

2. **Diplomatic Communications:**

   – Embassies and consulates use quantum encryption to secure sensitive diplomatic cables and negotiations.

3. **Satellite Communication:**

   – Quantum-encrypted satellite links protect global

communications from interception and espionage.

2. Intelligence Sharing

- **Secure Data Exchange:**

  – Quantum encryption facilitates secure data sharing among allied nations, intelligence agencies, and military branches.

- **Protecting Sources and Methods:**

  – Ensures that classified information about intelligence sources and methods remains inaccessible to adversaries.

3. Critical Infrastructure Protection

Quantum encryption strengthens the cybersecurity of critical infrastructure, including energy grids, transportation networks, and water systems.

1. **Supervisory Control and Data Acquisition (SCADA):**

   – Quantum-encrypted SCADA systems ensure secure monitoring and control of industrial processes.

2. **Supply Chain Security:**

   – Protects the integrity of military and government supply chains, ensuring authenticity and preventing tampering.

4. Quantum-Resistant Encryption for Stored Data

- **Classified Archives:**

  – Post-quantum cryptographic algorithms safeguard stored classified data from future quantum decryption attacks.

- **Cloud Security:**

  – Government cloud systems incorporate hybrid encryption frameworks combining classical and quantum methods.

QUANTUM-RESISTANT FRAMEWORKS FOR NATIONAL DEFENSE

To safeguard against quantum computing threats, national defense strategies must incorporate quantum-resistant frameworks that combine quantum encryption with robust infrastructure.

1. Quantum-Enhanced Secure Networks

National defense requires the establishment of quantum-secure communication networks that integrate QKD and quantum-safe algorithms.

1. **Military Communication Networks:**

   – Establish quantum-encrypted links between bases, command centers, and operational units.

2. **Integrated Government Networks:**

   – Ensure seamless and secure communication between federal, state, and local agencies.

2. Defense Against Quantum Threats

1. **Post-Quantum Cryptography:**

   – Deploy quantum-resistant cryptographic algorithms (e.g., lattice-based cryptography) to secure national defense systems.

2. **Quantum-Secure Cyber Defense:**

– Protect against cyberattacks targeting government systems using hybrid quantum-safe firewalls and intrusion detection systems.

3. Quantum-Resistant Key Management

1. **Centralized Key Management:**

– National agencies manage and distribute quantum-secure keys using centralized systems protected by QKD.

2. **Decentralized Key Distribution:**

– Distributed key management frameworks ensure redundancy and resilience against physical and cyber threats.

4. Real-Time Threat Detection

Quantum encryption supports real-time monitoring and detection of security threats, ensuring rapid response and mitigation.

1. **Quantum-Secure IoT:**

– IoT devices used in military and government applications are protected with lightweight quantum encryption.

2. **Advanced Persistent Threat (APT) Defense:**

– Quantum-enhanced AI systems detect and neutralize APTs targeting national defense systems.

• •

ETHICAL AND GEOPOLITICAL IMPLICATIONS

The adoption of quantum encryption in military and government applications raises important ethical and geopolitical considerations.

1. Ethical Implications

1. **Escalation of the Security Arms Race:**

   - The deployment of quantum encryption could intensify the cybersecurity arms race, with nations vying to outpace each other in quantum technologies.

2. **Privacy Concerns:**

   - Governments must balance the need for quantum encryption with citizens' rights to privacy, ensuring transparency and oversight.

3. **Dual-Use Technology Risks:**

   - Quantum technologies could be repurposed for offensive cyber operations, raising ethical dilemmas about their deployment.

2. Geopolitical Implications

1. **Strategic Advantage:**

   - Nations leading in quantum encryption gain a strategic advantage in defense, intelligence, and diplomacy.

2. **Global Power Dynamics:**

– Quantum encryption could shift the balance of power, with technologically advanced nations dominating global security.

3. **International Collaboration:**

– Collaboration on quantum encryption standards and technologies could foster trust and reduce the risk of conflict.

3. The Role of International Organizations

1. **Standardization Efforts:**

– Organizations like NATO and the United Nations must work to establish global standards for quantum encryption in defense.

2. **Non-Proliferation of Quantum Technologies:**

– Ensure that quantum encryption and related technologies do not fall into the hands of malicious actors or rogue states.

• •

CASE STUDIES

1. China's Quantum Military Communications

- **Scenario:**

  – China has developed a quantum-secure military communication network incorporating QKD and satellite-based quantum encryption.

- **Implementation:**

  – The network links command centers, mobile units, and intelligence facilities, ensuring secure communication even in contested environments.

- **Impact:**

  – Demonstrates the feasibility of large-scale quantum encryption deployment in national defense.

2. Quantum Encryption in NATO

- **Scenario:**

  – NATO has initiated pilot projects to integrate quantum encryption into its secure communication networks.

- **Implementation:**

  – Hybrid frameworks combining QKD with post-quantum cryptography are tested in joint military exercises.

- **Impact:**

  – Strengthens interoperability among member states while addressing the quantum threat.

3. U.S. Department of Defense Quantum Initiatives

- **Scenario:**

    - The U.S. Department of Defense has prioritized quantum encryption research to secure classified communications and infrastructure.

- **Implementation:**

    - Partnerships with private-sector quantum companies to develop and deploy QKD-enabled systems.

- **Impact:**

    - Accelerates the adoption of quantum-safe technologies across military and government agencies.

• •

CHALLENGES AND FUTURE DIRECTIONS

Challenges

1. **Cost of Implementation:**

   – Quantum encryption systems, such as QKD networks, are expensive to deploy and maintain.

2. **Technical Expertise:**

   – Limited availability of experts skilled in quantum technologies hinders rapid adoption.

3. **Scalability:**

   – Extending quantum-secure networks across large, distributed defense systems remains challenging.

Future Directions

1. **Miniaturization of Quantum Devices:**

   – Advances in quantum hardware will make encryption systems more accessible and cost-effective.

2. **Standardization and Collaboration:**

   – International cooperation on quantum encryption standards will facilitate widespread adoption and interoperability.

3. **AI-Enhanced Quantum Security:**

   – Integration of AI with quantum encryption systems will enable proactive threat detection and response.

CONCLUSION

Quantum encryption is set to revolutionize military and government security, providing unbreakable protection against emerging threats. By integrating quantum encryption into secure communications, intelligence sharing, and critical infrastructure, nations can safeguard their interests in an increasingly complex geopolitical landscape. However, addressing the ethical and geopolitical implications of this technology will be critical to ensuring its responsible deployment.

CHAPTER 14: HARDWARE FOR QUANTUM ENCRYPTION

Quantum encryption relies on cutting-edge hardware to harness the principles of quantum mechanics for secure communication. This chapter explores the essential components of quantum encryption hardware, including photonic devices, quantum processors, and detectors. It also examines the current market solutions, their applications, and the emerging trends shaping the future of quantum hardware.

• •

ESSENTIAL QUANTUM HARDWARE COMPONENTS

The hardware used in quantum encryption systems is critical for generating, transmitting, and detecting quantum states. These components ensure the functionality and reliability of quantum encryption protocols, such as Quantum Key Distribution (QKD).

1. Photonic Devices

Photonic devices are fundamental to quantum encryption as they manipulate and transmit photons, the carriers of quantum information.

1. **Single-Photon Sources:**

   –   Emit individual photons, which encode quantum information.

   –   Key Technologies:

   - **Weak Coherent Sources:** Lasers attenuated to approximate single-photon states.

   - **True Single-Photon Emitters:** Quantum dots and nitrogen-vacancy centers in diamonds.

   –   Applications:

   - Essential for QKD systems to ensure secure key exchange.

2. **Beam Splitters and Polarizers:**

- Beam splitters direct photons into multiple paths, creating superposition states.

- Polarizers encode information by altering photon polarization, crucial for protocols like BB84.

3. **Waveguides:**

- Integrated photonic waveguides guide photons with minimal loss, enabling scalable quantum circuits.

2. Quantum Processors

Quantum processors perform computations and operations on quantum states. In the context of quantum encryption, they play a role in complex key management and secure communication protocols.

1. **Quantum Chips:**

- Miniaturized processors that execute quantum operations using superconducting circuits or trapped ions.

- Examples:

  • IBM's superconducting quantum processors.

  • IonQ's trapped-ion quantum chips.

- Applications:

  • Advanced cryptographic operations, including quantum-safe key generation.

2. **Photonic Quantum Processors:**

- Utilize photonic qubits for performing operations, suitable for integration with optical communication systems.

3. Quantum Detectors

Detectors are critical for measuring quantum states with high precision and minimal error, ensuring the integrity of quantum communication.

1. **Avalanche Photodiodes (APDs):**

–   Widely used in QKD systems.

–   Detect single photons with high sensitivity.

–   Limitations:

  •   Higher dark count rates (false positives) compared to advanced detectors.

2. **Superconducting Nanowire Single-Photon Detectors (SNSPDs):**

–   Offer near-perfect efficiency and extremely low dark counts.

–   Operate at cryogenic temperatures.

–   Applications:

  •   Long-distance QKD and satellite-based quantum encryption.

3. **Transition Edge Sensors (TES):**

–   Highly sensitive photon detectors with precise energy resolution.

–   Ideal for applications requiring detailed photon state measurements.

• •

CURRENT MARKET SOLUTIONS

The quantum hardware market is rapidly evolving, with numerous companies and research institutions developing innovative solutions for quantum encryption.

1. Single-Photon Sources

- **ID Quantique:**

  – Offers true single-photon sources optimized for QKD applications.

- **Quandela:**

  – Specializes in quantum dot-based photon emitters for scalable quantum systems.

2. Quantum Detectors

- **Single Quantum:**

  – Manufactures SNSPDs for high-performance quantum communication.

- **Quantum Opus:**

  – Provides cryogenic photon detection systems tailored for research and commercial use.

3. Integrated Photonics

- **PsiQuantum:**

  – Develops integrated photonic circuits for scalable quantum computing and encryption.

- **Xanadu:**

– Focuses on photonic quantum processors with applications in quantum cryptography.

4. QKD Systems

- **ID Quantique:**

  – Offers complete QKD solutions, including photon sources, detectors, and key management systems.

- **Toshiba Quantum Key Distribution:**

  – Provides fiber-based QKD systems optimized for secure communication networks.

• •

FUTURE TRENDS IN QUANTUM ENCRYPTION HARDWARE

As quantum technology evolves, hardware development is focused on improving performance, scalability, and accessibility.

1. Miniaturization

- **Trend:**

    – Quantum hardware is becoming smaller and more energy-efficient, enabling integration into compact devices.

- **Example:**

    – On-chip photon sources and detectors for portable QKD systems.

2. Satellite-Based Quantum Communication

- **Trend:**

    – Deployment of quantum communication satellites to overcome the distance limitations of fiber-based QKD.

- **Example:**

    – China's Micius satellite demonstrated intercontinental QKD.

3. Quantum Repeater Development

- **Trend:**
  - Quantum repeaters are being developed to extend the range of QKD by mitigating signal loss and noise.

- **Future Impact:**
  - Enables secure communication across global distances.

4. Integration with Classical Systems

- **Trend:**
  - Hybrid systems combining quantum and classical components are gaining traction.

- **Applications:**
  - Quantum-secure data centers and hybrid encryption frameworks.

5. Cost Reduction

- **Trend:**
  - Advances in manufacturing techniques are driving down the costs of quantum hardware.

- **Example:**
  - Mass production of integrated photonic chips.

6. AI Integration

- **Trend:**
  - Artificial intelligence is being used to optimize the performance of quantum hardware.

- **Applications:**
  - Dynamic error correction in quantum detectors and adaptive photon routing.

• •

CHALLENGES IN HARDWARE DEVELOPMENT

Despite significant advancements, quantum hardware faces several challenges:

1. **Cost and Accessibility:**

   – High costs of quantum hardware limit widespread adoption.

2. **Operational Complexity:**

   – Many components, such as SNSPDs, require cryogenic environments.

3. **Standardization:**

   – Lack of standardized hardware interfaces hinders interoperability.

4. **Scalability:**

   – Scaling quantum systems for global communication networks remains a technical hurdle.

• •

CONCLUSION

Quantum encryption hardware forms the backbone of secure communication systems, enabling the implementation of QKD and other quantum-safe protocols. Essential components like photonic devices, quantum processors, and detectors are advancing rapidly, with market solutions addressing diverse applications. As future trends drive miniaturization, cost reduction, and integration with classical systems, quantum encryption hardware will become increasingly accessible, paving the way for widespread adoption. Overcoming the current challenges in scalability and standardization will be critical to realizing the full potential of quantum-secure communication.

CHAPTER 15: SOFTWARE FRAMEWORKS FOR QUANTUM ENCRYPTION

Quantum encryption, while grounded in advanced hardware, relies heavily on software frameworks to implement and manage its protocols effectively. These frameworks provide the tools for researchers and developers to design, test, and deploy quantum-secure systems. This chapter explores open-source quantum encryption libraries, guides the development of custom encryption software using popular Python libraries like Qiskit and Cirq, and discusses integrating quantum encryption APIs into existing systems.

• •

OPEN-SOURCE QUANTUM ENCRYPTION LIBRARIES

Open-source quantum encryption libraries provide accessible tools for implementing quantum cryptographic protocols. These libraries are essential for prototyping, testing, and deploying quantum encryption systems.

1. Qiskit (IBM)

- **Overview:**

    - Qiskit is an open-source quantum computing framework developed by IBM.

    - It provides tools for quantum algorithm development, including quantum cryptography.

- **Features:**

    - Supports simulation and execution on IBM Quantum's hardware.

    - Libraries for cryptographic algorithms and quantum key distribution (QKD) protocols.

- **Use Cases:**

    - Developing QKD simulation models and exploring post-quantum algorithms.

2. Cirq (Google)

- **Overview:**

  – Cirq is Google's open-source quantum computing library.

  – Designed for creating and simulating quantum circuits, including cryptographic protocols.

- **Features:**

  – Easy integration with Google's Quantum AI platform.

  – Tools for creating hybrid quantum-classical cryptographic solutions.

- **Use Cases:**

  – Testing the integration of quantum and classical encryption techniques.

3. ProjectQ

- **Overview:**

  – A lightweight framework focused on modular and efficient quantum computing.

- **Features:**

  – Integration with multiple quantum hardware backends.

  – Tools for implementing quantum-safe encryption schemes.

- **Use Cases:**

  – Prototyping lightweight quantum encryption protocols.

4. Quantum Cryptography Library (QuCryptox)

- **Overview:**

  – A specialized library for quantum cryptographic protocols.

- **Features:**

  - Pre-built QKD protocol implementations like BB84 and E91.

  - Support for quantum and classical hybrid systems.

- **Use Cases:**

  - Rapid development and testing of QKD systems.

5. PyQuil (Rigetti)

- **Overview:**

  - PyQuil is a Python library for quantum programming, developed by Rigetti Computing.

- **Features:**

  - High-level API for quantum algorithm development.

  - Integration with Forest, Rigetti's quantum cloud platform.

- **Use Cases:**

  - Developing quantum encryption software optimized for Rigetti hardware.

• •

DEVELOPING CUSTOM ENCRYPTION SOFTWARE

Developing custom quantum encryption software requires an understanding of quantum principles and the tools to translate these concepts into functional systems. Python libraries like Qiskit and Cirq provide a powerful foundation for building such software.

1. Setting Up the Environment

1. **Install Required Libraries:**

   – Use Python package managers like pip to install libraries such as Qiskit or Cirq.

   – Example:

   bash

   ```
   pip install qiskit cirq
   ```

2. **Configure Quantum Backends:**

   – Connect to quantum hardware or simulators, such as IBM Quantum or Google Quantum AI.

2. Developing Quantum Key Distribution (QKD)

Example: Implementing BB84 Protocol with Qiskit

1. **Quantum State Preparation:**

–   Encode qubits in random states:

python

```
from qiskit import QuantumCircuit
import random


qc = QuantumCircuit(1, 1)
state = random.choice(['0', '1', '+', '-'])  # Randomly
select state
if state == '1':
    qc.x(0)  # Apply X gate
elif state == '+':
    qc.h(0)  # Apply H gate
qc.measure(0, 0)
```

2. **Transmission and Measurement:**

–   Simulate photon transmission and measure results:

python

```
from qiskit import Aer, execute


backend = Aer.get_backend('qasm_simulator')
job = execute(qc, backend, shots=1)
result = job.result()
print("Measurement Result:", result.get_counts())
```

3. **Key Reconciliation:**

–   Use classical communication to align bases and derive shared keys.

3. Post-Quantum Cryptographic Algorithms

Develop post-quantum algorithms like lattice-based encryption using libraries like SciPy and NumPy.

1. **Lattice Key Generation:**

python

```
import numpy as np

def generate_lattice_key():
    matrix = np.random.randint(0, 2, (4, 4))
    private_key = np.linalg.inv(matrix)
    return matrix, private_key

public_key, private_key = generate_lattice_key()
print("Public Key:", public_key)
```

2. **Encryption and Decryption:**

–   Use lattice operations to secure messages.

4. Hybrid Encryption Solutions

Develop hybrid frameworks combining quantum and classical encryption using APIs like Cirq for quantum operations and PyCrypto for classical encryption.

1. **Quantum Key Exchange:**

–   Use Cirq to implement QKD.

2. **Classical Data Encryption:**

–   Encrypt data with the shared key using AES-256.

• •

INTEGRATING QUANTUM ENCRYPTION APIS

APIs for quantum encryption simplify the integration of quantum technologies into existing systems, allowing developers to focus on application-specific functionality.

1. IBM Quantum API

1. **Overview:**

   – Provides cloud access to IBM's quantum processors and Qiskit libraries.

2. **Use Cases:**

   – Develop applications integrating QKD and quantum-safe encryption.

2. Rigetti Quantum Cloud API

1. **Overview:**

   – Access Rigetti's quantum hardware and software ecosystem via PyQuil.

2. **Use Cases:**

   – Implement hybrid encryption schemes leveraging Rigetti's quantum services.

3. ID Quantique Quantum APIs

1. **Overview:**

   – APIs for integrating QKD into enterprise applications.

2. **Use Cases:**

– Secure cloud storage, VPNs, and financial transactions.

4. Quantum Encryption SDKs

1. **Overview:**

– SDKs from companies like Toshiba and QuintessenceLabs provide pre-built tools for quantum encryption.

2. **Use Cases:**

– Deploy end-to-end quantum-secure communication solutions.

• •

FUTURE TRENDS IN QUANTUM ENCRYPTION SOFTWARE

1. Simplification of Quantum Development

- **Trend:**
    - Development of higher-level APIs and user-friendly libraries.

- **Impact:**
    - Lowers the barrier to entry for developers without deep quantum expertise.

2. Integration with Emerging Technologies

- **Trend:**
    - Combining quantum encryption with AI and blockchain for advanced applications.

- **Example:**
    - AI-driven optimization of quantum cryptographic protocols.

3. Standardization of Quantum APIs

- **Trend:**
    - Establishing industry standards for quantum encryption software.

- **Impact:**

    – Facilitates interoperability across platforms and devices.

4. Cloud-Based Quantum Services

- **Trend:**

    – Expansion of cloud services offering quantum encryption as a service (QEaaS).

- **Example:**

    – Cloud platforms providing pre-configured quantum-secure APIs.

• •

CONCLUSION

Software frameworks for quantum encryption bridge the gap between theoretical quantum mechanics and practical applications. Open-source libraries like Qiskit and Cirq empower developers to create custom encryption solutions, while APIs streamline the integration of quantum technologies into existing systems. As quantum encryption software evolves, the focus will shift toward standardization, accessibility, and integration with emerging technologies, ensuring widespread adoption and robust security.

CHAPTER 16:
BUILDING QUANTUM-
RESISTANT
SYSTEMS TODAY

With the emergence of quantum computing, organizations must act now to future-proof their systems against potential quantum threats. Transitioning to quantum-safe infrastructure is critical to maintaining security in the face of quantum capabilities. This chapter outlines a roadmap for adopting quantum-resistant systems, provides guidance on adapting current infrastructure to incorporate quantum encryption, and presents a scalable framework for both small businesses and enterprise-level implementation.

• •

ROADMAP FOR TRANSITIONING TO QUANTUM-SAFE INFRASTRUCTURE

Transitioning to quantum-resistant systems involves a structured, phased approach to ensure minimal disruption while achieving long-term security.

1. Assessment Phase

1. **Vulnerability Analysis:**

   – Identify critical systems that rely on classical encryption vulnerable to quantum attacks (e.g., RSA, ECC).

   – Focus on areas like communication, data storage, and authentication.

2. **Data Sensitivity Audit:**

   – Categorize data based on sensitivity and retention periods.

   – Prioritize quantum-safe solutions for long-term sensitive data.

3. **Infrastructure Review:**

   – Evaluate hardware, software, and network components for compatibility with quantum-safe technologies.

2. Strategy Development

1. **Risk Mitigation Plan:**

   – Develop a risk mitigation strategy that outlines quantum-resistant practices.

2. **Budget Allocation:**

   – Allocate resources for training, hardware upgrades, and software development.

3. **Standard Compliance:**

   – Align with emerging quantum-safe standards from organizations like NIST or ETSI.

3. Pilot Phase

1. **Small-Scale Implementation:**

   – Deploy pilot projects for quantum-safe solutions in controlled environments.

   – Example: Implementing Quantum Key Distribution (QKD) for securing internal communications.

2. **Testing and Feedback:**

   – Test for performance, scalability, and integration issues.

   – Gather feedback to refine deployment strategies.

4. Full Deployment

1. **Gradual Rollout:**

   – Transition critical systems to quantum-resistant protocols in stages.

2. **Employee Training:**

   – Provide training programs to ensure staff can manage and operate quantum-safe systems.

3. **Ongoing Monitoring:**

- Continuously monitor systems for vulnerabilities and adapt as quantum technologies evolve.

5. Maintenance and Upgrades

1. **Regular Audits:**

   - Perform periodic audits to ensure systems remain quantum-safe.

2. **Technology Updates:**

   - Keep pace with advancements in quantum encryption and post-quantum cryptography.

3. **Incident Response:**

   - Develop protocols to respond to potential breaches or vulnerabilities.

• •

ADAPTING CURRENT SYSTEMS TO INCORPORATE QUANTUM ENCRYPTION

Existing systems can be adapted to incorporate quantum encryption without requiring a complete overhaul. The following steps enable organizations to integrate quantum-safe technologies into their current infrastructure.

1. Hybrid Encryption Approach

1. **Concept:**

   – Combine classical and quantum encryption to ensure compatibility and security during the transition.

2. **Implementation:**

   – Use QKD for secure key exchange while retaining classical encryption (e.g., AES-256) for data encryption.

3. **Advantages:**

   – Leverages existing infrastructure while introducing quantum security.

2. Post-Quantum Cryptography Integration

1. **Algorithm Replacement:**

–   Replace vulnerable algorithms (e.g., RSA, ECC) with post-quantum cryptographic algorithms such as lattice-based, code-based, or hash-based cryptography.

2. **Examples:**

–   Deploy NTRUEncrypt or Kyber for secure key exchange.

–   Use SPHINCS+ for quantum-safe digital signatures.

3. Infrastructure Upgrades

1. **Hardware Integration:**

–   Incorporate quantum encryption hardware such as single-photon sources, detectors, or quantum repeaters where needed.

2. **Quantum-Safe Gateways:**

–   Upgrade network gateways to handle QKD-secured communication.

4. Software Modifications

1. **API Integration:**

–   Integrate quantum encryption APIs from providers like IBM Quantum, ID Quantique, or Rigetti into existing software.

2. **Middleware Development:**

–   Develop middleware to facilitate communication between classical and quantum systems.

5. Network Security Enhancements

1. **Secure Channels:**

–   Establish quantum-encrypted communication channels for sensitive data transfers.

2. **Authentication Systems:**

–   Implement quantum-resistant authentication protocols to replace outdated systems.

FRAMEWORK FOR SMALL BUSINESSES AND ENTERPRISE-LEVEL IMPLEMENTATION

The transition to quantum-safe systems must be scalable to accommodate the unique needs of small businesses and large enterprises.

1. Small Business Implementation

1. **Key Challenges:**

   – Limited budgets and technical expertise.

   – Dependence on third-party service providers.

2. **Recommended Framework:**

   – **Adopt Post-Quantum Solutions:**

     • Use cost-effective post-quantum cryptographic libraries for encryption and key management.

   – **Leverage Cloud-Based Quantum Encryption Services:**

     • Opt for quantum encryption-as-a-service (QEaaS) platforms to avoid the need for in-house quantum hardware.

   – **Secure Communication Tools:**

- Upgrade to quantum-safe VPNs and messaging systems for secure internal and external communication.

– **Employee Training:**

- Provide basic training on quantum-safe practices and tools.

2. Enterprise-Level Implementation

1. **Key Challenges:**

– Complexity of existing infrastructure.

– High volume of sensitive data and distributed systems.

2. **Recommended Framework:**

– **Dedicated Quantum Security Team:**

- Establish a team responsible for planning and overseeing the quantum-safe transition.

– **Phased Implementation:**

- Begin with high-priority systems such as financial data, intellectual property, and classified communication.

– **Deploy QKD Networks:**

- Establish QKD-secured communication links between data centers, headquarters, and branch offices.

– **Integrate Quantum Gateways:**

- Use quantum-secure gateways for managing secure communication across hybrid classical-quantum networks.

– **Collaboration with Vendors:**

- Partner with quantum hardware and software providers to implement tailored solutions.

CASE STUDIES

1. Government Infrastructure Modernization

- **Scenario:**

    - A government agency transitions its classified communication systems to quantum-safe encryption.

- **Implementation:**

    - Deployed QKD links for secure communication between government facilities.

    - Replaced RSA with lattice-based encryption for document storage.

- **Outcome:**

    - Achieved long-term security for sensitive data and reduced risk of quantum threats.

2. Financial Institution's Hybrid Framework

- **Scenario:**

    - A multinational bank integrates quantum encryption into its operations.

- **Implementation:**

    - Used QKD for inter-branch communication.

    - Upgraded customer authentication systems with quantum-resistant algorithms.

- **Outcome:**

    - Enhanced data security while maintaining compliance with international regulations.

CONCLUSION

Building quantum-resistant systems today requires a proactive and phased approach to transition from classical to quantum-safe infrastructure. By following a structured roadmap, adapting existing systems, and implementing scalable frameworks, organizations of all sizes can protect their operations against quantum threats. As quantum technology evolves, continued innovation and collaboration will ensure that these systems remain secure and effective in the quantum era.

CHAPTER 17: TESTING AND VALIDATING QUANTUM ENCRYPTION SYSTEMS

As quantum encryption systems move from theoretical development to real-world deployment, rigorous testing and validation are critical to ensuring their robustness, security, and reliability. This chapter explores the standards and protocols for testing quantum encryption systems, the role of simulated attacks in evaluating system robustness, and the importance of certification and compliance with international standards.

• •

STANDARDS AND PROTOCOLS FOR TESTING QUANTUM ENCRYPTION

Testing quantum encryption systems requires adherence to standardized methodologies that ensure consistent evaluation and comparability across implementations. These standards cover key aspects such as performance, security, and interoperability.

1. International Standards for Quantum Encryption

1. **ETSI Quantum-Safe Standards:**

    –   The European Telecommunications Standards Institute (ETSI) has developed guidelines for quantum-safe cryptography and Quantum Key Distribution (QKD).

    –   Focus:

        •   Protocol testing.

        •   Integration with classical systems.

        •   Interoperability across platforms.

2. **NIST Post-Quantum Cryptography Standards:**

    –   The National Institute of Standards and Technology (NIST) is leading efforts to standardize post-quantum cryptographic algorithms.

- Focus:

  - Algorithm security under simulated quantum attacks.

  - Performance benchmarks for practical applications.

3. **ISO/IEC Standards:**

- The International Organization for Standardization (ISO) and the International Electrotechnical Commission (IEC) provide standards for cryptographic security and testing.

- Examples:

  - ISO/IEC 19790: Security requirements for cryptographic modules.

  - ISO/IEC 15408: Common criteria for information technology security evaluation.

2. Testing Protocols

1. **Functional Testing:**

- Verifies that quantum encryption systems perform as expected.

- Examples:

  - Correct key generation and exchange using QKD.

  - Accurate implementation of post-quantum cryptographic algorithms.

2. **Performance Testing:**

- Evaluates the efficiency and scalability of quantum encryption systems under varying workloads.

- Metrics:

  - Key generation rate.

  - Data throughput.

- Latency in communication.

3. **Interoperability Testing:**

– Ensures seamless integration of quantum encryption systems with existing classical infrastructure.

– Focus:

- Compatibility with communication protocols (e.g., TLS, IPsec).

- Consistency across hardware and software platforms.

• •

SIMULATING ATTACKS TO EVALUATE ROBUSTNESS

Simulating attacks is a critical part of testing quantum encryption systems. These simulations help identify vulnerabilities and validate the system's resilience against adversarial threats, including both classical and quantum-based attacks.

1. Types of Simulated Attacks

1. **Classical Attacks:**

   –   Brute force, man-in-the-middle (MITM), and side-channel attacks.

   –   Test the system's resilience to conventional hacking techniques.

2. **Quantum Attacks:**

   –   Exploit the capabilities of quantum computers to break cryptographic algorithms.

   –   Example: Using Shor's algorithm to factorize RSA keys.

3. **Channel Attacks in QKD:**

   –   **Intercept-Resend Attacks:**

       •   Simulates an eavesdropper intercepting and resending photons in QKD.

   –   **Trojan Horse Attacks:**

- Injects extra photons to gather information about the quantum states.

- **Photon Number Splitting (PNS) Attacks:**

- Exploits multi-photon emissions to extract information.

2. Simulation Tools and Techniques

1. **Quantum Simulators:**

- Tools like IBM Quantum Experience and Cirq provide environments for simulating quantum encryption systems and attacks.

2. **Cryptanalysis Frameworks:**

- Software like SageMath is used to simulate cryptographic attacks on post-quantum algorithms.

3. **Hardware-in-the-Loop Testing:**

- Combines software simulations with real quantum hardware to evaluate end-to-end system security.

3. Metrics for Robustness Evaluation

1. **Error Rates:**

- Measure the system's ability to detect and correct errors introduced by attacks.

2. **Eavesdropping Detection:**

- Evaluate the effectiveness of quantum systems in identifying adversarial interference.

3. **Key Distillation Efficiency:**

- Test the system's ability to produce a usable key despite attack attempts.

• •

CERTIFICATION AND COMPLIANCE WITH INTERNATIONAL STANDARDS

Certification provides assurance that quantum encryption systems meet established security and performance criteria. Compliance with international standards ensures interoperability and global acceptance.

1. Certification Processes

1. **Common Criteria (CC):**

   – A globally recognized certification framework for evaluating IT security.

   – Focus:

     • Cryptographic modules and their implementation in quantum systems.

2. **FIPS 140-3:**

   – A U.S. government standard for cryptographic modules, including quantum-safe implementations.

   – Focus:

     • Physical security.

     • Algorithmic robustness.

3. **ETSI Certification:**

– ETSI offers certification for QKD systems to validate their implementation and interoperability.

2. Compliance Guidelines

1. **GDPR Compliance:**

– Ensure that quantum encryption systems used for data storage and communication adhere to data protection regulations like the General Data Protection Regulation (GDPR).

2. **Industry-Specific Standards:**

– Financial Services: PCI DSS compliance for quantum-secure payment systems.

– Healthcare: HIPAA compliance for quantum-secure medical data.

3. Benefits of Certification

1. **Trust and Confidence:**

– Certified systems provide assurance to stakeholders about their security and reliability.

2. **Market Adoption:**

– Certification facilitates broader adoption by ensuring compatibility and compliance.

3. **Regulatory Acceptance:**

– Simplifies adherence to government and industry regulations.

• •

CASE STUDIES

1. Quantum Key Distribution System Validation

- **Scenario:**

    – A telecommunications company tests a QKD system for securing 5G communication.

- **Process:**

    – Conducted simulated attacks, including PNS and MITM attacks.

    – Certified the system under ETSI standards.

- **Outcome:**

    – Achieved compliance, leading to deployment in national infrastructure.

2. Post-Quantum Cryptography Algorithm Evaluation

- **Scenario:**

    – A financial institution evaluates lattice-based encryption for securing customer transactions.

- **Process:**

    – Used cryptanalysis frameworks to simulate quantum attacks.

    – Validated algorithm performance under NIST guidelines.

- **Outcome:**

    – Successfully integrated quantum-resistant algorithms into payment systems.

CHALLENGES AND FUTURE DIRECTIONS

Challenges

1. **Evolving Standards:**

   – Rapid advancements in quantum technology outpace standardization efforts.

2. **Complex Testing Environments:**

   – Simulating realistic quantum attacks requires sophisticated tools and expertise.

3. **Cost of Certification:**

   – Certification processes can be resource-intensive, particularly for small organizations.

Future Directions

1. **Automation in Testing:**

   – Development of automated tools for testing and validation.

2. **Global Standards Harmonization:**

   – Collaboration among international organizations to create unified standards.

3. **Advanced Simulation Platforms:**

   – Use of AI-driven simulators for dynamic and adaptive testing scenarios.

• •

CONCLUSION

Testing and validating quantum encryption systems are essential to ensuring their security, performance, and compliance with international standards. By adopting standardized protocols, simulating a variety of attacks, and achieving certification, organizations can deploy quantum encryption systems with confidence. As quantum technologies continue to evolve, ongoing advancements in testing methodologies and standards will play a critical role in maintaining the robustness of quantum-safe systems.

CHAPTER 18:
THE FUTURE
OF QUANTUM
ENCRYPTION

Quantum encryption, rooted in the principles of quantum mechanics, is poised to redefine data security in the coming decades. As the field evolves, advancements in research, the integration of artificial intelligence, and speculative applications promise to expand its scope and capabilities. This chapter explores emerging trends in quantum encryption, the potential role of artificial intelligence in quantum systems, and future technological milestones that could shape the trajectory of quantum security.

• •

TRENDS IN QUANTUM ENCRYPTION RESEARCH

Quantum encryption is advancing rapidly, with researchers exploring new methods, technologies, and applications to enhance security and efficiency.

1. Beyond Quantum Key Distribution (QKD)

QKD has been the cornerstone of quantum encryption, but future research is diversifying its applications:

1. **Quantum Digital Signatures:**

   – Leveraging quantum states to create tamper-proof digital signatures, ensuring message authenticity and non-repudiation.

2. **Quantum Secure Direct Communication (QSDC):**

   – Developing protocols for direct communication of messages without intermediate key generation.

3. **Quantum Random Number Generation (QRNG):**

   – Enhancing the quality and speed of random number generation for cryptographic systems.

2. Post-Quantum Cryptography Integration

1. **Hybrid Protocols:**

   – Combining quantum encryption with post-quantum cryptography to achieve robust security against both classical and quantum attacks.

2. **Algorithm Optimization:**

–   Research into efficient post-quantum algorithms like lattice-based and hash-based cryptography to reduce computational overhead.

3. Scalable Quantum Networks

1. **Quantum Internet:**

–   Establishing global quantum networks that enable secure communication between distant parties using quantum teleportation and entanglement swapping.

2. **Quantum Repeaters:**

–   Overcoming the distance limitations of QKD through advanced quantum repeater technology.

4. Miniaturization of Quantum Hardware

1. **On-Chip Quantum Systems:**

–   Integration of quantum encryption hardware into compact devices, enabling secure communication for IoT and mobile platforms.

2. **Portable QKD Devices:**

–   Development of lightweight and cost-effective QKD systems for widespread adoption.

● ●

THE POTENTIAL ROLE OF ARTIFICIAL INTELLIGENCE IN QUANTUM SYSTEMS

Artificial intelligence (AI) and machine learning (ML) are emerging as transformative tools in the development and optimization of quantum encryption systems.

1. Enhancing Quantum Key Distribution

1. **Dynamic Error Correction:**

   – AI algorithms can optimize error correction protocols in real-time, improving QKD efficiency and reliability.

2. **Adaptive Protocols:**

   – ML models can dynamically adjust encryption protocols based on network conditions and potential threats.

2. Advanced Threat Detection

1. **Eavesdropping Detection:**

   – AI-powered analytics can identify patterns indicative of eavesdropping attempts in QKD systems.

2. **Quantum Channel Monitoring:**

   – Real-time monitoring of quantum channels using AI to detect anomalies or environmental disturbances.

3. Quantum Algorithm Design

1. **Optimization of Post-Quantum Algorithms:**

    – AI can streamline the development of post-quantum cryptographic algorithms, balancing security and computational efficiency.

2. **Discovering New Protocols:**

    – Generative AI models can explore novel quantum encryption protocols beyond current human designs.

4. Integration with Quantum Hardware

1. **Quantum Device Calibration:**

    – AI algorithms can fine-tune quantum hardware settings for optimal performance and minimal noise.

2. **Hybrid Systems:**

    – Coordination between quantum and classical systems using AI for seamless operation in hybrid encryption frameworks.

• •

SPECULATIVE APPLICATIONS AND TECHNOLOGICAL MILESTONES

The future of quantum encryption extends beyond current applications, encompassing speculative uses and groundbreaking milestones.

1. Global Quantum Networks

1. **Quantum Internet Infrastructure:**

    –   Connecting nations through a secure quantum communication backbone, transforming global cybersecurity.

2. **Interplanetary Quantum Communication:**

    –   Extending quantum networks to support secure communication in space exploration and colonization.

2. Integration with Emerging Technologies

1. **Quantum-Blockchain Synergy:**

    –   Quantum encryption could secure blockchain transactions, ensuring immutability and resistance to quantum attacks.

2. **Secure AI Systems:**

    –   Protecting AI models and data using quantum

encryption to prevent tampering or theft in critical systems.

3. Biomedical and Genetic Data Security

1. **Secure Genomic Data Storage:**

   –   Quantum encryption ensures the privacy of genetic information in research and healthcare.

2. **Quantum-Secure Remote Surgery:**

   –   Protecting real-time communication between surgeons and robotic systems in remote medical procedures.

4. Decentralized Identity Management

1. **Self-Sovereign Identity (SSI):**

   –   Quantum encryption enables tamper-proof, decentralized digital identities for secure authentication.

2. **Cross-Border Digital Credentials:**

   –   Facilitating secure and seamless verification of digital credentials across nations.

5. Quantum-Driven Encryption Standards

1. **Universal Quantum Protocols:**

   –   Development of globally accepted quantum encryption standards to unify cybersecurity practices.

2. **Dynamic Encryption Paradigms:**

   –   Quantum encryption systems that adapt to emerging threats in real-time.

• •

TECHNOLOGICAL MILESTONES IN QUANTUM ENCRYPTION

Future milestones in quantum encryption will mark the transition from niche applications to global ubiquity.

1. Affordable Quantum Hardware

- **Milestone:**

  – Achieving cost-effective production of quantum encryption hardware for consumer and enterprise use.

- **Impact:**

  – Democratization of quantum encryption technology.

2. Fully Functional Quantum Internet

- **Milestone:**

  – Deployment of a fully operational quantum internet connecting cities and continents.

- **Impact:**

  – Revolutionizing global communication and cybersecurity.

3. Standardization of Quantum Cryptographic Protocols

- **Milestone:**

  – Adoption of universal standards for quantum-safe and

hybrid encryption frameworks.

- **Impact:**

  –   Ensuring compatibility and interoperability across industries.

4. Quantum-AI Hybrid Systems

- **Milestone:**

  –   Development of integrated quantum and AI systems for enhanced cryptographic capabilities.

- **Impact:**

  –   Transforming data security and intelligence analysis.

5. Mass Adoption in Critical Sectors

- **Milestone:**

  –   Quantum encryption becomes standard in healthcare, finance, government, and military applications.

- **Impact:**

  –   Unprecedented levels of data security and privacy.

• •

CHALLENGES AND CONSIDERATIONS

While the future of quantum encryption is promising, several challenges must be addressed:

1. **Ethical Implications:**

   – Balancing security with privacy and preventing misuse of quantum technologies.

2. **Global Inequities:**

   – Ensuring equitable access to quantum encryption across nations and organizations.

3. **Technological Overlap:**

   – Navigating the integration of quantum encryption with other disruptive technologies like AI and blockchain.

· ·

CONCLUSION

The future of quantum encryption holds immense potential to redefine the security landscape, from enhancing global communication to safeguarding critical systems. Advancements in quantum research, the integration of AI, and speculative applications such as a quantum internet and secure decentralized identities will drive the next generation of cryptographic innovation. While challenges remain, ongoing research and collaboration across disciplines will ensure that quantum encryption becomes a cornerstone of global security in the quantum era.

CHAPTER 19: ETHICAL AND SOCIETAL IMPLICATIONS OF QUANTUM ENCRYPTION

Quantum encryption promises unparalleled security for communications and data. However, its adoption raises profound ethical and societal implications, particularly concerning privacy, surveillance, and the equitable distribution of technology. As quantum encryption becomes integral to our digital infrastructure, it is essential to address these issues to ensure that the technology benefits all of humanity. This chapter explores the balance between privacy and surveillance, strategies to prevent misuse, and the importance of global cooperation in the quantum age.

• •

BALANCING PRIVACY AND SURVEILLANCE IN A QUANTUM-SECURE WORLD

Quantum encryption strengthens privacy by making data nearly impervious to eavesdropping and hacking. However, this heightened security also has the potential to empower malicious actors and hinder legitimate law enforcement efforts.

1. Privacy Empowerment

1. **Strengthened Individual Rights:**

    –   Quantum encryption ensures that personal communications, financial transactions, and sensitive data remain private and secure from third-party surveillance.

2. **Protection Against Authoritarianism:**

    –   Provides a shield for individuals and organizations in oppressive regimes, enabling free expression and dissent without fear of retribution.

2. Challenges for Surveillance

1. **Legitimate Law Enforcement Needs:**

    –   Quantum encryption complicates lawful interception, a tool often used to combat terrorism, cybercrime, and organized crime.

2. **Undetectable Communications:**

- Malicious actors, including criminals and terrorist groups, could exploit quantum encryption to conduct activities undetected.

3. Ethical Considerations

1. **Universal Right to Privacy:**

- Quantum encryption can uphold privacy as a fundamental human right, aligning with principles in documents like the Universal Declaration of Human Rights.

2. **Balance with Security:**

- Developing frameworks to balance the need for individual privacy with collective security responsibilities.

4. Potential Solutions

1. **Quantum Backdoors:**

- Carefully regulated backdoors for legitimate law enforcement use. However, these must be approached cautiously to prevent abuse.

2. **Transparency and Oversight:**

- Public and independent oversight committees to ensure that quantum technologies are not misused by governments or corporations.

3. **Encrypted Lawful Interception:**

- Explore quantum-safe mechanisms for lawful access without compromising overall encryption strength.

. . . .

PREVENTING MISUSE OF QUANTUM ENCRYPTION TECHNOLOGIES

The unparalleled security offered by quantum encryption could be exploited by bad actors, including rogue states, organized crime, and cybercriminals. Proactively addressing misuse is essential to maintaining global security.

1. Risks of Misuse

1. **Shielding Criminal Activity:**

   – Quantum-secure communication channels could be used to coordinate illegal activities without fear of interception.

2. **Cybercrime Asymmetry:**

   – Criminal organizations might adopt quantum encryption faster than law enforcement, creating a security gap.

3. **State-Sponsored Misuse:**

   – Governments could use quantum encryption to mask illicit activities or develop undetectable cyber-espionage capabilities.

2. Ethical Guidelines for Development

1. **Ethical Design Principles:**

- Developers of quantum encryption systems should adhere to principles prioritizing societal well-being and transparency.

2. **Dual-Use Concerns:**

- Quantum encryption technologies should be designed to prevent misuse, especially in sensitive applications like military communication.

3. Mechanisms to Prevent Misuse

1. **International Regulation:**

- Establish global agreements regulating the development, deployment, and use of quantum encryption technologies.

2. **Technology Monitoring:**

- Develop AI-powered monitoring systems to identify potential misuse of quantum-secure systems without violating privacy rights.

3. **Sanctions and Enforcement:**

- Impose strict penalties for misuse of quantum encryption technologies, backed by international coalitions.

• •

GLOBAL COOPERATION IN THE QUANTUM AGE

Quantum encryption's impact extends beyond national borders, requiring international collaboration to establish equitable and secure systems.

1. The Need for Cooperation

1. **Cross-Border Security:**

   – Global interconnectedness necessitates secure international communication channels based on quantum encryption.

2. **Preventing Quantum Divides:**

   – Avoid a scenario where only technologically advanced nations benefit from quantum encryption, leaving developing countries vulnerable.

2. Collaborative Frameworks

1. **International Quantum Encryption Standards:**

   – Establish universal standards for quantum encryption to ensure compatibility and equitable access.

2. **Global Research Consortia:**

   – Promote joint research initiatives among nations to develop and deploy quantum encryption technologies inclusively.

3. **Shared Quantum Infrastructure:**

– Develop shared resources like global quantum networks to facilitate secure communication across borders.

3. Bridging the Quantum Divide

1. **Technology Sharing:**

– Encourage developed nations to share quantum encryption technologies with less technologically advanced countries.

2. **Capacity Building:**

– Invest in education and training programs to build quantum expertise globally.

3. **Public-Private Partnerships:**

– Leverage partnerships between governments, academia, and the private sector to democratize quantum encryption access.

4. Geopolitical Challenges

1. **Techno-Nationalism:**

– Nations may prioritize domestic quantum advancements, creating barriers to international cooperation.

2. **Quantum Arms Race:**

– Competition to achieve quantum supremacy could lead to secrecy and a lack of trust among nations.

3. **Policy Divergence:**

– Different approaches to privacy, surveillance, and technology regulation could complicate cooperation.

5. International Oversight

1. **Role of Global Organizations:**

– Entities like the United Nations and World Economic

Forum can mediate discussions and establish norms for quantum encryption.

2. **Quantum Ethics Council:**

–   Form an independent global body to oversee the ethical use of quantum encryption technologies.

· ·

CASE STUDIES

1. Quantum Encryption in International Diplomacy

- **Scenario:**

  – Nations leverage quantum-secure communication channels for sensitive diplomatic negotiations.

- **Impact:**

  – Strengthens trust between nations while protecting against cyber-espionage.

- **Challenge:**

  – Ensuring equitable access to quantum encryption for all participating countries.

2. Balancing Privacy and Surveillance in Counterterrorism

- **Scenario:**

  – Governments implement quantum encryption for public communication while enabling limited lawful interception for counterterrorism.

- **Impact:**

  – Enhanced public trust and effective security measures.

- **Challenge:**

  – Preventing misuse of surveillance capabilities.

3. Technology Sharing Across Borders

- **Scenario:**

  – A coalition of nations collaborates on quantum encryption research and shares the resulting technologies with developing countries.

- **Impact:**
  - Reduces the global quantum divide and strengthens international cybersecurity.

- **Challenge:**
  - Overcoming geopolitical rivalries.

• •

CONCLUSION

Quantum encryption offers immense potential to protect privacy, enhance security, and transform communication. However, its adoption also brings ethical challenges, particularly in balancing privacy with surveillance, preventing misuse, and ensuring equitable access. Global cooperation is essential to navigate these complexities and harness the transformative power of quantum encryption responsibly. By fostering collaboration, establishing robust ethical frameworks, and addressing the risks of misuse, the global community can ensure that quantum encryption serves as a force for good in the quantum age.

CONCLUSION: EMBRACING QUANTUM SECURITY

Quantum encryption stands at the forefront of technological innovation, promising to revolutionize the way we secure communications and data. Throughout this book, we have explored the theoretical underpinnings, practical applications, challenges, and future directions of this transformative technology. As we conclude, it is essential to reflect on the key insights gained, issue a call to action for stakeholders, and reaffirm the promise of quantum encryption as the cornerstone of secure communication in the quantum era.

• •

SUMMARY OF KEY INSIGHTS FROM THE BOOK

1. The Foundations of Quantum Encryption

- **Quantum Mechanics as the Basis:**

  - Principles like superposition, entanglement, and the observer effect form the core of quantum encryption.

- **Quantum Key Distribution (QKD):**

  - Protocols like BB84 and E91 ensure secure key exchange by leveraging quantum states' inherent properties.

2. The Urgency of Quantum Security

- **Impending Quantum Threats:**

  - Quantum computers, with their ability to break traditional encryption algorithms, pose a significant risk to current cryptographic systems.

- **Transition to Quantum-Safe Systems:**

  - Post-quantum cryptography and hybrid frameworks provide a roadmap for securing existing infrastructure.

3. Practical Applications

- **Cross-Industry Adoption:**

  - From secure messaging and VPNs to quantum-resistant blockchain and IoT systems, quantum encryption is reshaping industries.

- **National Security:**

  – Military and government agencies are leveraging quantum encryption to protect critical communications and infrastructure.

4. Challenges and Opportunities

- **Technical and Ethical Hurdles:**

  – Balancing privacy with surveillance, preventing misuse, and addressing cost and scalability issues are critical challenges.

- **Advancing Technology:**

  – Innovations in hardware, software, and integration with AI are unlocking new possibilities for quantum encryption.

5. Global Cooperation and Societal Impact

- **Bridging the Quantum Divide:**

  – Ensuring equitable access to quantum encryption technologies is essential for global security.

- **Ethical Deployment:**

  – Establishing transparent standards and regulations will prevent misuse and foster trust in quantum technologies.

• •

CALL TO ACTION FOR BUSINESSES, GOVERNMENTS, AND INDIVIDUALS

The quantum era is fast approaching, and proactive steps are needed to prepare for its transformative impact.

1. For Businesses

- **Assess Vulnerabilities:**

    - Conduct audits to identify systems and data that are vulnerable to quantum threats.

- **Adopt a Phased Approach:**

    - Transition to quantum-safe infrastructure incrementally, starting with critical systems.

- **Invest in Training:**

    - Equip employees with the knowledge and skills to implement and manage quantum encryption technologies.

2. For Governments

- **Lead by Example:**

    - Governments must adopt quantum encryption to secure public infrastructure and communications.

- **Foster Innovation:**

- Invest in research and development to drive advancements in quantum encryption.

- **Collaborate Internationally:**

  - Work with global organizations to establish standardized protocols and share best practices.

3. For Individuals

- **Understand the Technology:**

  - Stay informed about quantum encryption and its implications for personal privacy and security.

- **Advocate for Privacy:**

  - Support policies and initiatives that prioritize ethical deployment and transparency in quantum technologies.

- **Prepare for Change:**

  - Recognize that quantum encryption will redefine how personal data and communications are secured in the future.

• •

THE PROMISE OF QUANTUM ENCRYPTION

Quantum encryption is more than a technological innovation; it represents a fundamental shift in how we think about security and trust in the digital age.

1. A New Paradigm of Security

- Quantum encryption provides unparalleled protection against both current and future threats. Its reliance on the immutable laws of quantum mechanics ensures that data remains secure, even in the face of evolving adversarial capabilities.

2. A Catalyst for Innovation

- As quantum encryption integrates with emerging technologies like AI, blockchain, and IoT, it will unlock new possibilities for secure and efficient systems across industries.

3. A Pillar of Global Stability

- By securing communications and critical infrastructure, quantum encryption can contribute to global peace and stability, reducing the risks of cyber warfare and espionage.

4. An Opportunity for Ethical Leadership

- The development and deployment of quantum encryption offer humanity a chance to prioritize ethical principles, ensuring that this powerful technology benefits all and safeguards fundamental rights.

• •

FINAL THOUGHTS

The quantum revolution is not a distant possibility but an imminent reality. Quantum encryption, with its promise of unbreakable security, stands as the vanguard of this transformation. However, the successful adoption of quantum encryption will require collaboration, foresight, and a commitment to ethical principles. By embracing quantum security today, businesses, governments, and individuals can build a resilient, secure, and equitable future, ensuring that the promise of quantum encryption is realized for generations to come.

www.ingramcontent.com/pod-product-compliance
Lightning Source LLC
Chambersburg PA
CBHW071449220526
45472CB00003B/740